The Violinist of
Auschwitz

The Violinist of
Auschwitz

Jean-Jacques Felstein

PEN & SWORD
HISTORY

Originally published by Éditions IMAGO in 2010 as
Dans l'Orchestre d'Auschwitz

First published in Great Britain in 2021 by
Pen & Sword History
An imprint of
Pen & Sword Books Ltd
Yorkshire - Philadelphia

ISBN 978 1 39900 281 3

Typeset by Mac Style
Printed and bound in the UK by CPI Group (UK) Ltd,
Croydon, CR0 4YY

MIX
Paper from
responsible sources
FSC® C013604

Pen & Sword Books Limited incorporates the imprints of Atlas, Archaeology,
Aviation, Discovery, Family History, Fiction, History, Maritime, Military,
Military Classics, Politics, Select, Transport, True Crime, Air World,
Frontline Publishing, Leo Cooper, Remember When, Seaforth Publishing,
The Praetorian Press, Wharncliffe Local History, Wharncliffe Transport,
Wharncliffe True Crime and White Owl.

For a complete list of Pen & Sword titles please contact

PEN & SWORD BOOKS LIMITED
47 Church Street, Barnsley, South Yorkshire, S70 2AS, England
E-mail: enquiries@pen-and-sword.co.uk
Website: www.pen-and-sword.co.uk

Or

PEN AND SWORD BOOKS
1950 Lawrence Rd, Havertown, PA 19083, USA
E-mail: Uspen-and-sword@casematepublishers.com
Website: www.penandswordbooks.com

Contents

Prologue   vii

Chapter 1   Hélène and Violette   1

Chapter 2   An Anniversary   22

Chapter 3   The Chaconne   34

Chapter 4   The Weight of Words   46

Chapter 5   The Orchestra   68

Chapter 6   Alma   79

Chapter 7   Hairdresser and Beauty Salon: "Paris-Beauté"   93

Chapter 8   Second Violin   101

Chapter 9   Tochter aus Elysium   112

Chapter 10 Polonaises   129

Chapter 11 The Dying Swan   147

Chapter 12 Sylvia   155

Epilogue   160
Members of the Women's Orchestra of Auschwitz   173
A Selection of Works from the Repertoire   177

Jean-Jacques Felstein, with his mother.

Prologue

Cologne, summer 1958

The sky is grey, streaked with mustard yellow. It's the colour of my nightmares. It is a nightmare. There are thousands of us huddled, naked and crowded against each other on an esplanade with no limits. Although out in the open air, a continuous wail among thousands of cries seems to be reflected by the polished walls of a huge bathroom. You're right behind me, within earshot: the only reassuring presence in my proximity. You don't speak to me; you look all around you, crazily. Maybe you don't even know that I'm here? A thrust exerted from who knows where pushes us en masse towards a metal portico, overlooking a staircase. Still huddled together, we go up, step by step, jostling with each other and shouting even more. As we ascend, my anxiety increases. The cries reach a deafening level. We advance down a corridor that leads to the void. Those who were before me have disappeared; you must have disappeared too. I have to launch myself into this emptiness and I see that the whole metallic structure we've climbed is nothing more than a gigantic diving board. Below is a swimming pool, tiled in white earthenware, with blue lines marking the swimmers' lanes. The colours are crisp, the lines are sharp. There's no water in the basin. We have to throw ourselves into it; we throw ourselves into it to kill ourselves …

I wake up out of breath. I'm alone, you're at work.

As a child, this dream was the first representation of mass destruction, our destruction by Nazism. This vision of disaster, as I'd built it, having no other details than those I'd gleaned from you, in my search for contact with you. You'd chosen not to tell me anything about what you'd suffered a few years before I was born. I had a lot of imagination at the time, but from what I felt through you, I already knew that this horror wasn't made up of horned demons, flying dragons or wolves frothing at the mouth: all the usual swarms that populate childish imaginations. Deep down, I knew that this disaster must've been a foolish, technological, anonymous and hygienic nightmare, just like the massacre and those who planned it.

Loyal to you down to the last fibre of my being, I realized that your inability to pay me any attention was creating a chasm between us over time. The interior destruction that you'd suffered was so complete that you didn't even have the words to think it, and *a fortiori* to tell me.

You'd witnessed it, you still bore the scars: a five-digit number, underlined by a downward-pointing triangle, tattooed on the outside of your left arm, 10 centimetres from the elbow joint. The blue-black number was quite small, but each stroke that made it was a cut containing unspeakable offences.

Also striking were the bad dreams that woke you up screaming, hallucinating, and that left my father powerless to calm you down. I knew we shouldn't talk about it. I had to wait a long time to understand that what allowed you to magically keep these nightmares away was sometimes the evening kiss that I gave you, whatever it cost me, whatever had happened between us during the day. Another factor that cemented our bond were the migraines that left you helpless and made you push anyone who tried to approach you as far away as possible. I couldn't get over this, so I suffered the same ailments: it was the only thing I could take from you without risking becoming too weak.

I'd known for a long time that you couldn't always be present and constantly available to me. I knew it would've been inappropriate to ask you for more than you gave me. From your behaviour and through what was tacitly implied around us, I clearly understood that I had no right to be frustrated. In light of what you'd suffered, my needs were paltry.

*   *   *

At that time we lived in a small detached house, the whole family together. The eyes of other family members – what I've always called your family – wanted to protect you and had the effect of separating us even more. Why? What right did they have to come between us, the three of us first, then the two of us later, after your divorce? Why did they have an opinion on us, and why did you allow them to have one? My expectations as a small child, no doubt a bit precocious, were too demanding, my pain too sharp for you to be able to do anything other than alternate between passivity and explosions of anger. Others, therefore, took care of me when you were too busy...

Not enough warmth and comfort when I needed it, not enough words to justify or explain. My childhood questions were obstinately refused, making your past and my origins taboo.

As far back as I can remember, I have the feeling of having been constantly on the alert, awaiting a vague catastrophe which, in the most benign of cases, would leave us separated from each other, and, in the worst case scenario, both of us dead. It was an event that couldn't be spoken of, and the weight of which you carried with you even before I came along.

I called for you and you didn't answer, or at least not enough. This frustration, so unsuitable and so well-hidden from those around us – weren't you a saint? – has undoubtedly marked me for my whole existence.

*   *   *

To this silence where you let me grow were added a few details of a standard 1950s interior: a portrait of a child and some books.

Drawn in red chalk and pastel on craft paper, the portrait was of a 3-year-old child, Lydia, standing at the edge of a beach in Knokke [Belgium]. The little girl is wearing a grey outfit. Her face shows full, red cheeks, framed by blonde hair cut in the style of the 1920s. She has the roundness of those little girls approaching the end of infancy. The artist was fairly unknown, but the painting was supposedly won by Lydia after being elected 'the most beautiful child on the beach' in the summer at the end of the "Belle Époque". Duly framed, it hung in the living room, along with the out-of-tune piano and the abominable more-or-less Flemish *Still Life with Pheasant* painting on the back wall, always in shadow. It was a room one only passed through 'so as not to damage anything'.

We also had about thirty novels: Alexandre Dumas' Musketeers trilogy, Louis Amédée Achard's *Les Coups d 'épée de Monsieur de la Guerche* and *Belle-Rose*, the complete works of the Comtesse de Ségur. Covered with blue or brown paper, the titles of the volumes were carefully inked on schoolboy labels in pen, making them look like loved and then neglected books. Unlike the portrait, they weren't kept in the living room, but had been stored in the back of a wooden cabinet that occupied an entire wall of the kitchen. These were "Aunt Lydia's books". I read them greedily, and treated them like relics. They were relics, but I didn't know it at the time.

So I had a portrait of a little girl, the books of a pre-adolescent girl, and the grown-up name, "Aunt Lydia". Three distinct ages for an otherwise mysterious person. She was very young to be anyone's aunt, and no one, you least of all, wanted to tell me who or where she was.

I couldn't make the link between Lydia and this opaque past until much later. I would first have to go through a series of particular disasters, and let a moment infuse the cataclysm that was affecting all of us, without my knowing it.

*   *   *

Forgive me for telling you so bluntly, you who suffered both, but the explosion of our family was as intense for me as the Nazi massacres. In the childish universe of which I was the uncertain centre, you and my father formed the retaining arc. It still wavered, the three of us weren't very strong, and your separation destroyed the little internal security I had left.

At the time I had nightmares full of fractures, ruptures and tears. In my dreams I looked for the two of you in burning cities, in ruins, and in permanently devastated landscapes. Your departure to Germany scattered what was left of me to the four winds. For that, just as for your separation, I wasn't prepared. You left as if you were fleeing something, while I was elsewhere, as they used to say, "in a camp". It was at a children's home – for Jewish children – on the Channel coast, where I encountered the notion of the Second World War for the first time. It was also the first time that I found myself alone.

I spent two months there in the fog, terrorized. My body was out of sorts: I was peeing in bed as if my life depended on it. I lost or had all my possessions stolen whenever I didn't give them to someone who asked for it nicely. I wondered when and by what chance I would see you again. The Germany you had joined, for you, for us, wasn't neutral, and vibrated in me harmonics of indefinite suffering. Yours, no doubt.

Your departure evoked exile too much. Our separation realized my recurring anxiety: a train carrying you away, and me with dangling arms, unable to escape, left behind on the platform forever.

I was able to start thinking about growing up again when it became clear I would regularly come to visit you in Cologne, where you had opened a cosmetic salon. To be alternately with my father and then with you forced me to live in two exclusive contexts. When I was 9 I had to cross half of Europe on my own to be with you. Nevertheless, I managed to find a little place to develop, and also gained the possibility of losing neither of you... As long as you were there at the station or at the airport to collect me, although I was never certain this would be the case.

Seeing the twin steeples of Cologne Cathedral approach, a sign that the journey's end was in sight, always brought me back to the same absurd question: 'Will she be there when I arrive? And if

Leaving for Cologne.

not, who'll help me get my suitcase off the luggage rack?' It was a little by this yardstick that I measured my height: there came a time when I was able to get off and carry this unfortunate suitcase by myself. My father provided me with a ticket before each trip on which was written in German: *My name is Jean-Jacques, my mother lives in Habsburgerring 18-20, her phone number is 23 22 01*. Thus fermenting the idea it was possible that you might not be there when I arrived…

It all came to light from a marble plaque at the entrance to my school and Chaplin's *The Great Dictator*. The plaque had been put up in memory of the pupils and their teachers who'd been deported in 1942, and from which no one had returned. In a family like ours, it was impossible for me not to have heard this simple word, "deportation". Admittedly, a silent pact had been implicitly concluded between all of you on the maternal side of the family. We weren't supposed to talk about "before", the people before, or what had happened to them, but that didn't stop the word from resurfacing now and again. Much later, I deduced that we probably concluded the pact when you, "Elsa-the-survivor", returned from Belsen, while neither your father, nor Lydia, her parents Rosa (my grandmother's older sister) and David, had returned from Auschwitz. Beyond the fact that it allowed you to rebuild your lives, which wasn't easy, this pact was also intended to protect me, the first to be born "after". Caught like the others in the family compact, I would gladly close my ears as soon as the word came up.

However, sometimes at family reunions I'd suddenly hear ten adults murmuring like children exchanging slightly dirty secrets. It was there that "the word" circulated and the names of Lydia and Rosa were whispered – never that of David, never that of your father. That was when I was sent to read elsewhere.

As "the word" gradually took over – deportation, where we never came back – snippets of these conversations I'd heard in spite of their efforts to hide them also began to take on meaning.

I intuitively understood what had happened to this "Aunt Lydia". She was known to me as "Aunt", not because she was an adult, and that as such I owed her respect, but because this eternally young little Lydia *could've been* an adult to whom I *could've* owed respect. I didn't know in detail how the promises carried by such a short life had been dashed. This little girl, who'd died without trace, symbolized the axe blow inflicted by Nazism on our history, the gaping hole in the story of our lineage. There was clearly a void that nothing could fill, a wound all the more painful in than it had never been spoken of.

The Great Dictator came out in Paris. Perhaps you'll take this as a simple posthumous tribute to the genius of Chaplin, but I have to say this: in my head he managed to make Tomania's Hynkel the "real one", while Hitler was the caricature. It was hard for me to see the swastika as a symbol of Nazism rather than the two crosses in a white circle worn on the armbands in Chaplin's film. Hynkel perfectly personified the man who screamed hatred and murder, and his Germanic belching failed to make me laugh. That film – which came out before the facts! – was for me the first "documentary" representation of the mechanisms of the Holocaust.

*   *   *

André Schwartz-Bart had just won the Goncourt prize for *The Last of the Just*, and our head teacher read us the final chapter of the book, the one where everyone is killed, men, women, children, in a gas chamber masquerading as a shower room. The description of their death in the darkness for all those people, all ages and sexes alike, was startling, and was the source of new nightmares for me. These were more vivid, more clinical, but they were no less scary.

At roughly the same time, a classmate, Didier, constantly spoke of a place he'd heard about in his family, the "Chvitz". He talked about it in the courtyard, at dinner, in class. We listened to some of it, fascinated. People died there after unspeakable tortures, and it was located neither in space nor time. Nevertheless, this 'Chvitz' existed somewhere. If this place was more real than Ali Baba's cave, Pitchipoi,[1] or the cyclops' lair in *The Odyssey* – Didier seemed to know what he was talking about – it was not so much what was said, but the memories it awakened in me. Memories that had been imbued at the same time as I was rocked by similar terrors.

Rather than telling my father about it, I waited to see you in Cologne to ask if you knew about this "Chvitz". A Belgian friend hearing me ask you the question made a well-known gesture: the thumbnail passing over the throat, and added a sickening sound from his mouth. 'Shhh!' you said, quickly and without question, thus confirming by default what my friend had said about it.

Imperceptibly, incomplete explanations were stuck end to end in a totally anarchic fashion; from Lydia to deportation, and from deportation to "Chvitz". I was beginning to grasp a detail you had passed on to me that made me a suspended death row inmate: I was Jewish.

I can tell you now that for a long time it was a dangerous weight on me: a trait to hide as much as possible. I still see myself in the streets of Cologne, a group of children trying to force me into a church, and me wondering if I should admit *why* I had no business there… Without knowing directly, I thus endorsed the threadbare defrocking of the ghetto Jew who, outside the walls, bowed his head under the insults, and arched his back under the blows.

In this contradictory and agonizing muddle, I still had to face the moment when world history and our family history collided. Of course, this happened in Germany.

* * *

---

1. The imaginary place where displaced Jews in France believed they would be deported to.

I still have trouble understanding your return to that country today. You were out of place. We often went there on vacation, of course, but as for settling there… You worked like a beast of burden. After all, launching a beauty salon called "Paris-Beauté" in Cologne was a difficult gamble. As time went on, I noticed an increasingly strong French accent in the German you spoke with your clients. You sprinkled your conversations with them with 'eh?' and 'non!'. I don't know if this was a deliberate and commercial choice on your part, or if you were marking some sort of distance between yourself and those to whom you were speaking.

Your only friends were French people, or at least French speakers. There was a profound ambiguity in your situation in Cologne. You were a long way away from your family, which must have been quite liberating as you could lead your life as you saw fit, without being judged by your relatives on your possible escapades. However, you didn't succeed in creating sufficient ties to the place in order to feel at home there. I knew this very position, both involved and distanced, was the same one you had towards me, and it is the one that I often had myself.

"Paris-Beauté" prospered honourably: the "little Frenchwoman" was beginning to be known in Cologne. While at first you lived there for economy's sake, or to be at work sooner – you slept on the baby blue sofa that was used in the waiting room during the day – you later had decent accommodation: accommodation where I could stay on my own and read when you were working. You didn't know how to introduce me to children my own age, and I didn't know how to make friends: I wasn't shy, I was almost wild. At first, I spent my days in the salon, bored, unable to do anything but try to grab you, even when you had to take care of a client. Since then, the soft and violently fragrant atmospheres of hair salons have depressed me: I still see myself, the only boy in the harem, vaguely disturbed by this languid femininity, too young to interest anyone, too foreign to exchange more than 'Guten Tag' or 'Danke schön' with fat ladies who came to be pampered.

Among your friends there is one, Ruth, who was very important to me. A German Jew, she had spent the war in hiding and was completely bilingual. With the possible exception of your friends from Belgium, Helene Wiernik[2] and Fanny Kornblum, and despite the fact that the two of you had followed completely different paths, she must undoubtedly have been the person closest to you. As short as you were, plump, with red hair and milky skin, she was tall, thin, brunette and tanned, whatever the season. She was pretty, funny, lively, sensitive, and had this faculty of knowing how to listen without judging. You finally had someone to confide in regarding your suffering, past or present.

You liked Ruth, and she liked you. I liked her too because you loved her, and she was the only adult I know who, at that time, looked up to me.

Your difficulty in settling in Germany wasn't only material and administrative: problems of a different nature also existed. You had spent part of your childhood in this country and had witnessed the rise of barbarism. You knew all the tones and registers of the German language: those of children's poetry and nursery rhymes, and those of the SS and bureaucrats. The language couldn't ring pleasantly in your ears.

Until the mid-1960s, Cologne still had traces of the war. They reminded you that the city hadn't been innocent when the barbarians were there, triumphant. Bullet traces in the stone, holes in the walls, houses in ruins, constructions that were too new. Traces on the men, aging, with yellow armbands on which three black dots arranged in a triangle indicated the invalid or the blind. I had read about it and already knew that, thirty years ago, this

---

2. The women of the orchestra are referred to throughout the work by the names they bore at the time of their deportation, mostly their maiden names. See table, p. 173.

combination of colours, black on a yellow background, indicated a fate of a completely different nature: it was the infamous and deadly stamp of the Jew. There was also that Germanic way used by adults and children, just to say 'hello', of clicking their heels and brutally bowing their heads forward, which always made me jump and seemed to repel you.

You must have been wondering what they had done fifteen years ago, those respectable little old men. I also wondered without asking the question openly, to you or to them.

Traces remained in people's minds, too. The whole of Germany was traumatized by swastikas and 'Juden Raus' (Jews Out!) daubed on the outside of the new synagogue in Cologne, shortly before its inauguration, located just over the other side of the square from where we lived.

* * *

The history was still there, I understood it when the play of *The Diary of Anne Frank* was performed in Germany. You wanted to see the play, and you wanted me to see it as well. My fluency in German at that time was more than basic, but before I even went to the theatre I knew I would be bored, and that I wouldn't understand a thing... Despite my vehement protests and, as far as I can remember, after a tough negotiation leading to a few movie shows, you managed to drag me out. As expected, I was very bored, but the rest of the play occurred between the two of us. You suddenly revealed to me that, like Anne, you had been deported to Bergen-Belsen, that you had contracted typhus, and that you had almost died there.

And so you had been in a place with this funny name where, at the same time, you could have met someone famous like Anne Frank, and died. Even for someone familiar with German – as I was – there was a peculiar form of dark exoticism in this kind of rhyme with four strong, rhythmic syllables: Ber-Gen-Bel-Sen. Can we call it trauma? This moment of revelation of a past, yet still active, horror, which I had always unconsciously perceived and whose words and those four rough syllables were beginning to outline?

One of my great pains is that the moment when you told me about this little part of you was the only time in your life when you told me about yourself. The only moment when a few words from you could allow me to begin to think about it all, instead of living it through nightmares. Full words, inhabited, affixed to a haze of impressions and completely heterogeneous fragments: Lydia, Nazism, your previous silence, Anne Frank, what else? What, in me, was an incoherent and inarticulate breeding ground, wasn't organized magically, however. But, instead of the previous chaos from which my anxieties rose in waves, something that I could lean on was then made apparent to me. It was you who finally revealed yourself in your integrity, because the things you hadn't told me before stood between us, barring any possibility of real dialogue. This unique moment of confidence will always make me regret what could have been, if you had chosen truth between us instead of silence.

I read a lot. *The Diary of Anne Frank*, initially, and then several times; perhaps I was vaguely hoping to find you there at the turn of a page? Then *Exodus* and *Mila 18* by Leon Uris. One spoke of the birth of the State of Israel, seen through the eyes of camp survivors. The other evoked the uprising in the Warsaw Ghetto. The main characters were identifiable and the "Chvitz" of my childhood became Auschwitz. I realized that in reality, the abomination in my childhood nightmare was lovable poetry.

That which had remained silent between us, I approached through novels and eye-witness accounts. It was no less evocative. The documents, so numerous today, were still rare: the first assembly of archives I heard about arrived in Cologne in 1960. It was called *Mein Kampf.* Very watered down, it had nevertheless caused a scandal when it was released but it was forbidden to those under sixteen years of age, like the last of the "naked" films of the time.

All this wasn't enough to explain your absence and our inability to communicate. *Our* inability, because it was becoming increasingly normal. My bulimia of reading about what had affected you so heavily, combined with the incipient inflation of speeches on the "concentration camp phenomenon", led me, without my noticing it, to put a certain distance between you and me. I integrated myself into the faceless mass of "deportees", thereby levelling out what made your story *before* so unique. My growing "intellectual" knowledge of the "experience" of the camps resolved the crucial question for me, the original question that's usually asked of parents: 'Who am I?' The answer, which I lived with for a very long time, too long, was always: 'I come from Auschwitz, my story began there, my life was woven there, my personality was built there, and my origin remains there.'

Once again, what tormented me overlapped the rest. I needed references, benchmarks. Not knowing who you really were, because the silence – yours and that of your family – still weighed over entire swathes of your life, all of which made mine, in the literal sense of the word, impossible. Before I could better understand what had happened to you, I had to overcome two major crises: adolescence, which was cataclysmic, and the year 1964.

In Cologne, your future seemed dark to you. You saw yourself aging and alone, and this vision frightened you. You wanted to rebuild a home and, above all, give life. If possible to a girl who, like the missing girl, would be called Lydia, as a final reparation for the past.

After a few painful failures, your family found you a husband – a father for the future Lydia – in a remote corner of the United States. When this project came to fruition, you probably didn't have the strength to talk to me about it face to face; you wanted others to present it to me, explain it to me and, in many ways, justify it to me.

I still see the four of us around the table in the family living room: the two of us, your mother and your stepfather. The latter began to ask me, jokingly, in your presence, what I would think if you remarried. You were silent, and showed little enthusiasm. It was so sad; like a scene from an Italian comedy. The world was upside down. In short, they were asking my consent for you to remarry and move 10,000 kilometres away from me.

From the start of the conversation, I already knew this was no joke and that the decision had probably already been made. With my insides like jelly, I still found myself saying that as long as I didn't lose you, I had no other option but to resign myself to it. So I was left with the prospect of seeing you only once a year, at best: in the early 1960s, a trip to America was a luxury. My inability, at the time, to complain or even acknowledge the low regard that people had of me still amazes and revolts me.

My consent was required for a marriage without passion, a "marriage of convenience". Helplessly, I raged against those "reasonable" people who couldn't stand you being free and running your life, and especially those who took you away from me. Thirty-five years later I still wonder if, secretly, you hoped I might resort to blackmail through an epileptic fit or an act of violence: something to help or to force you to make up your own mind, for you to show you had to resist because I, too, was at stake. I kept quiet and can't forgive myself, but my rage was also directed against you, as well as against me. In addition to your migraines, perhaps I had also acquired from you this ability to always put myself second?

So you left and got married. When I came to see you, in the summer of '63, my sister Lydia had just been born. We were far apart: we hardly saw each other, let alone talked. I went for a walk, alone. I went to the movies or bowling, alone. I read in my room.

You were tired, you weren't recovering well from childbirth, and you also had to take care of the little one. You lived with your husband and daughter – I didn't consider her as my sister yet – in a small house in a town in the far reaches of the American Midwest: Frederick, Oklahoma, 350 kilometres southwest of Dallas, Texas: a long street, 3,000 inhabitants, 30 churches, a cinema and a swimming pool, then the desert. As far as I could tell, the main social activity seemed to be visiting neighbours, eating barbecue and admiring their respective refrigerators.

I didn't understand you, and the only way you were able to show your affection towards me was by giving me gifts. So I have a pen, my "Parker", which you gave me, and which I still use.

In the United States.

Your smart and funny husband seemed to care about you. He was kind and attentive to me, but when I looked at you there was nothing there.

Following on from our failed meeting in Cologne, this unsuccessful reunion in America seemed to me to be quite normal. We couldn't have known it would be the last. As I left to take my flight home, you were sad and distraught and so I put my arm around your shoulders. In consolation, I think I reminded you that I'd be back – not that it was my decision! The words jostled in my head and I held a tight ball of sobs back down in my throat, as you probably did, too. When it was time to say goodbye my tongue twitched and I said, 'see you later'. It still hurts not to have been able to admit to you, even then, how much your absence weighed on me, and how much more I wanted to know you.

*   *   *

Cologne, July 1964

> *The locomotive calls for the latecomers, my mother is ready to go. To get to the platform, she has to go through a long hallway. She's at the entrance and I reach out to her. She walks down the hall, while I try to hold her back. She loses shape the further away she is. I call her, she turns and smiles vaguely.*

Ruth told me of Elsa's death and burial in Wichita Falls, Texas, while I was on vacation with her in Cologne. Despite my efforts to forget her, I had known for several months that she had cancer. She told me in her letters that she had to go for "ray" sessions several times a week because she had many cysts on her body. My father, for once up to the task, had tried to prepare me for the outcome. The event was too serious and too big for me to grasp, and so I mentally cancelled it.

Once the telegram announcing "the event" was actually in my hands, there were no more pretences. As much as I wished with all my might that those words had never been said, nothing helped. It had happened.

As everyone undoubtedly does in these circumstances, I tried to conjure her in my mind and found that all I had left was the sound of her voice in my ear. I believe that while I still held onto her inside me, I definitely lost the image of her at this point. Perhaps, by dying, I was confusedly angry with her for abandoning me so definitively? Her death 10,000 kilometres away from me made her abstract. In regards to Elsa's death, I was unable to mourn or find peace until thirty years later, when I saw a photograph of her grave in my sister's papers.

But that night, my first as an "orphan", what kept the madness at bay was a crazed anger: the same reasonable people who, rightly or wrongly, I partially blamed for this mess, also wanted me to give prayers of thanks, to thank God for letting her die, she who had never intentionally been mean to anyone. Ruth also wanted me to do it; I don't know if it was to occupy my mind, to respect their wishes, or because she believed in it.

Outraged and sickened by the ridiculousness of it all, and cursing everyone except Ruth, I did, and it was on this occasion, and for the last time, I saw the interior of a synagogue: all those grotesque, chanting old men rocking back and forth like psychotics really did nothing to resuscitate a faith that was long lost to me anyway.

* * *

My mother Elsa's premature death had paradoxical effects. Transfigured, she became a saint, a magical and untouchable character. She seemed to have taken the symbolic place in my family that the little rosy-cheeked Lydia had previously occupied, and an invisible circle formed around her, dedicated to the maintenance of the flame. I wasn't a part of this circle. Her mother and father-in-law were the organizers and excluded me from it, including when they sobbed loudly without restraint, all the time. Did they show others their suffering? This frozen, disembodied object, which was presented as my late mother, was only her imaginary mausoleum. I didn't want it, I hated it; it concealed everything that could have been alive and spontaneous about her, it made the secret that remained even heavier, and kept me at a distance from her after her death, just as it had done during her lifetime.

Partly as a teenage reaction, but above all so as not to lose a connection to Elsa that proved more meaningful as I grew older, I rejected these simplistic representations outright, and those who promoted them. I realized pretty quickly that a compact, imprecise mass of guilt held it all together, for everyone in the family, me included. The guilt of not having had to survive the way she had to. The guilt of not having gone there when so many others hadn't returned: Lydia, Rosa, David, my grandfather, and others, on whom the silence which weighed down became more and more untenable.

I was no better or of a "purer being" than the others. I fought alone, with rage and without any fervour to keep a memory of Elsa alive in me that didn't correspond at all to this icon in its golden frame.

Regarding her deportation, I understood more and more from what I *learned*, from reading testimonies, and from photographs and films. The obscene film shot in Belsen by English reporters, showing heaps of corpses being carted like rubbish by mechanical shovels, did the rounds. I asked myself the question that arguably plagued the lives of all the children of survivors in secret: 'What did she have to do to survive this?' During an argument with my grandmother, revolving around the issue of inheritance, I heard her mutter that Elsa 'hadn't rotted in Auschwitz for me to do whatever I wanted with it'. The inheritance was my share of a pension which

Elsa received from the federal government as compensation for war damage. In German it was called *Wiedergutmachung*. Literally, 'the act of making everything good again'.

Beyond the elegance of my grandmother's words, I couldn't tell if 'Auschwitz' was used in the generic sense, to indicate "deportation" in general, or if Elsa had actually been detained there. While mentally taking note, I didn't elaborate too much on it. To imagine Elsa in this context was both too violent for me and too degrading for her.

*   *   *

It was through a succession of haphazard deductions and improbable associations that I came to a more nuanced and calming representation of my mother. It was done in stages, just like decompression.

The first element was a contradiction I noticed when people spoke to me about her. I understood from my father and Elsa's brothers that she was a good musician, yet I had never seen her play any instruments. She had a good musical ear, and sang well. It was at home, through her, that I had listened to my first classical music records, Smetana's *The Moldau*, Beethoven's *Fifth*, and Mendelssohn's *Concerto in E minor*. I had learned that she had had a violin, and I even took it over to her in the United States in a scratched and dented case, following Lydia's birth.

We experienced, she and I, a unique moment with this violin, during which I almost approached a constitutive, fundamental truth: a moment that I let pass, of course. We were in my room when she opened the case, took out the instrument, and started to tune it. The violin was old and didn't look very good and, the tuning being awkward, it took a few minutes. The strings were worn, the bow poorly stretched, and the trigger guard needed to be replaced. She performed all the rituals of a musician: the gestures of adjustment were made automatically because they had been repeated a 100 times before. Once this was over, she played a few notes. She was tense, uncertain. It didn't sound right, it had to be re-tuned over and over again. Motionless, I watched her do it, feeling that something decisive was happening. After one last unsuccessful attempt, she sighed, put the instrument back in the case, closed it definitively, and went to see Lydia, who was crying in the next room. The moment of possible dialogue between us had, once again, passed me by.

Questions swirled around in my head. How can someone *have been* a good musician? In other words, how was it possible for someone to stop making music for so long that they could no longer play? I wasn't a musician yet at that time, but I had discovered music long before. I just couldn't understand how Elsa could have stopped doing something so important to her without missing it. Unable to ask her the question openly, I nevertheless felt that, for her, playing the violin must somehow be linked to unbearable memories. Without my realizing it, a whole network of associations was set in motion, ranging from the violin to deportation, then to the restorative function that the birth of my sister had played. However, the answers didn't fall into place like the pieces of a puzzle. On the contrary, they constituted a patchwork where nothing corresponded; beyond the gaps that remained in our relationship, my mother was no longer just this self-evident presence that was there to look after a child. She was no longer just secretive, silent, physically and emotionally absent. She was also complex, contradictory and incoherent. She was becoming opaque to me.

*   *   *

Based on this inconsistency, over the years I have built a representation for myself, and it's a photograph that probably got me started. It shows an inmate from a concentration camp. His hands are tied, and he's standing on a miserable cart that may as well have been a toy in a previous life, as it's nothing more than a crate on wheels. The cart is being pulled along by other detainees, all dressed in striped uniforms. Their hunched backs and knees punctuate the uniform and even threaten to slip through. Their hair is cropped short and they all look alike. The one perched on the cart, however, has his eyes turned more inward, his face is more downturned than that of his comrades. The caption for the photograph simply states it's an inmate who has been sentenced to death by hanging, being taken to his place of execution.

For its sheer existence, this photograph is already a crime against humanity: only a camp guard would have had the idea to "immortalize" the scene, and I wonder what man might want to keep such a thing as a souvenir?

A further obscenity is added to the scene: detainees are stood in military formation behind the cart, in rows of five, Prussian style. It's a parade. There are violins, an accordion, a few flutes. One of the musicians has his eyes closed, as if trying to put more feeling into what he's playing. We don't know the piece of music they're performing. Apart from the one with closed eyes, the faces are expressionless. Are they playing Chopin's *Funeral March*, transforming the condemned man into a living corpse? Are they playing a modern song, or a catchy tune to celebrate the event?

As a musician myself, having started to play the guitar after my mother died, I perhaps feel the monstrosity of this connection between music and death administered in this way even more.

I remembered, however, that there were people in these camps who played music, and everything started to organize and fall into place in my head. The question of knowing what prostitution, moral or physical, my mother had to indulge in to come back from that place where people didn't return from, finally had a tolerable answer: to come back from *there*, she must have played the violin.

While not facilitating my own relationship with music, this conjecture had the merit of giving me, if not a coherent one, at least a more calming vision of Elsa. A simple representation with which I could coexist.

Not all of this work happened quickly, or smoothly. These associations, which seem logical in their sequence, were based most of the time on impressions, on facts as inconsistent as wisps of straw, and were only supported by my desire to understand what had been missing between Elsa and me. The answers to these questions that were so essential to me didn't emerge from some cornucopia. Each new link took its place in the chain because the electric shock, nausea or cold sweat I had experienced served as a criterion of truth. These shocks and the great calm that seized me physically afterwards warned me of the resonance inside myself of what I had discovered about *her*.

*   *   *

When one of my uncles, the family musician, told me that my mother had been part of the Birkenau women's orchestra, he virtually said 'how did you not know?' Vaguely outraged and a little contrite, he confirmed what I was thinking, also telling me that I was probably the last member of the family to know about it. As late as it was – I was 35 years old, and Elsa had died nearly a quarter of a century before – my uncle's words, combined with the personal work I had undertaken, in many ways set me on the road to my release.

The Nazis had wanted to reshape the past by physically annihilating several generations, by destroying the places where the victims had lived, by destroying the traces of their births in civil records, and of their deaths in cemeteries. Their ultimate crime was to transfer to Auschwitz the family narrative and the memory of the survivors' descendants, *those who, like me, were born anyway, despite their efforts.*

By an unconscious journey, the meanders of which I can in no way transcribe, this confirmation of my intuition had the effect of authorizing me to give up recognizing myself at Auschwitz, allowing it to be part of my identity and my origins. My fascination with 'returning' to this abject and sterile place of industrial death became unnecessary.

For me, Elsa was now no longer an enigmatic and supernatural being, she (re)became a woman born of a man and another woman, whose much-needed story could be sought in the rubble, in Lodz, Dortmund, Cologne or Wichita Falls. She was no longer just a "deportee", defined in all of her actions by two unspoken years. Beyond the nightmares of her nights and of mine, despite the position of sainthood and martyrdom that the members of her family always gave her, I could, I can, still love her, still be angry with her for our misunderstandings, and still miss her: after all, she was just my mother.

Chapter 1

Hélène and Violette

The women's orchestra (artist unknown).

Paris, February 1995

Once again, everything has completely fallen apart for me. Ruth has sent me a book from Cologne which she obtained through complicated channels. Published in Belgium, it focusses on a character who has become a legend: a young woman deported to Birkenau, Mala Zinetbaum. Deported from Belgium, Mala was soon appointed as a *Läuferin* (messenger) in Birkenau, then as an interpreter. Testimonies about her make her out to be a particularly endearing character, one of those figures that we can't forget. As an interpreter, she had access to a number of facilities in the camp, including food and clothing, and was extraordinarily dedicated to helping as many inmates as possible, Belgians in particular, but not just by giving them a piece of bread, or a transfer to a less exhausting *Kommando*, a better fitting pair of shoes, or simply a smile or a compassionate word: something that could, at the right time, prevent someone from letting go, from letting themselves die.

With the help of her counterpart in the men's camp, Edek Galinski, she escaped Birkenau. However, they were captured after weeks of a Nazi manhunt across Europe. During the 'ceremony' of his execution by hanging, Mala had violently rebelled against Edek's tormentors: slapping one, the foul Tauber, she then slashed her veins with a razor blade. These "ceremonies" were used by the Nazis to set an example – there was no escaping a *Lager* – and all the detainees would have been there to witness Mala's execution and therefore witnessed her revolt as well.

This book about Mala is made up of memories and statements from a number of survivors. One of them, Hélène, recalls her arrival in Auschwitz and her meeting with a young girl she described as 'neat, with a kerchief on her head, and laced boots'. Her name was Elsa Miller: you, my mother. She recounted how you had taken her out of the mass of deportees in quarantine, to shelter her a little, by coming to fetch her to join the orchestra.

I had already met Hélène during a visit that we, Elsa and I, had paid her in Hasselt in 1961. I remember that her daughter, Danielle, had played Bach's *Prelude in C* on the piano, the one which makes up the harmonic base of Gounod's *Ave Maria*.

The relative balance that I had found, the feeling that this part of your life I had put into the attic of my own mind, was upset again by these few lines.

What Hélène said meant more to me than the family regurgitations I had suffered since your death thirty years before. They had the character of a memory, precious and vague at the same time. But they didn't proceed from a desire to appropriate what you represent, a feeling of theft constantly renewed and actualized by each evocation – or summons – of you in front of me in our family. Reading you described as "neat" made me see you again, in the morning, when you were getting ready to leave for work, when you were doing your makeup, always neat and tidy, and it gave me back the precision of your gestures, that little mascot who bravely returns to combat every day. It was your presence in my memory, transposed onto the backdrop of Birkenau, concrete, precise and without the trappings of passing time, which I was hit with head on.

It was easy for me to reconnect with Hélène through the editors of the book. One failed act, however, nearly ruined everything. Instead of giving the intermediaries my personal telephone number, I gave my work number … as if to prevent her from finding me.

A whole stream of images haunts me again. Watchtowers, electrified barbed wire, blocks seen from an airplane, lined up like a giant Lego set. A procession of shadows that crawl around, dressed in striped uniforms, and you, standing out against this background, with a few rare locks of hair carefully hidden by your white scarf. I imagine your appearance in what I see as an enclosure, where the new arrivals are huddled together in quarantine. It's a waking nightmare that takes shape. But a nightmare lived by Hélène and you. Yet for the first time, I had found someone who had *seen* you in this context, who had lived with you through those two almost unspeakable years, someone who loved you, too.

Completely contradictory thoughts flood through me, right at the same time as I'm on the telephone with Hélène. Will it hurt her to tell me about you? The time that was stolen from you there, those sensations, those feelings, those events that you couldn't, didn't know how, or didn't want to share with me, will Hélène be able to transmit them to me without too much damage to herself?

But I'd also just been hit in the stomach by the need to pass on the history of your group so that it didn't become lost. The story of the women's orchestra at Birkenau is so extraordinary that it almost takes hold of me physically. Meeting Hélène and talking about it, these two desires overlapping and intertwining. But would Hélène grant me the right to know your secrets, something that was always forbidden to me during your lifetime? Is it almost a rape, a taboo, that I'm asking her to condone?

I don't need to display feats of eloquence: Hélène seems to understand my request without saying. She points me in the direction of one of her friends in Paris, Violette Zylberstein, who was with the two of you in the orchestra and has a particularly keen memory.

When I think about these first contacts, I realize how much I really am my mother's son. My request concerning you had to be presented in this convoluted form; I was interested in your life back in those days – how strange! how easy to say! – but impossible to proceed other than by articulating it in an incomparably complex project, in which my quest for you can succeed. Nothing less than the story of a group of forty-five women, of which you were one of the most secretive. Will I be old enough, one day, to allow myself to look for you, first and foremost you, simply for myself?

Paris, March 1995
This is my first meeting with Violette. We greet each other formally, but she also gives me a kiss to welcome me. Small, lively, and energetic, she smokes like a chimney. Her voice is a bit hoarse, veiled, and the sometimes surprising images she constructs, the flowery if not very PC language she uses, make me appreciate her immediately. She is a "little old lady" who isn't afraid to say what she wants. She immediately considered me to be a valid interlocutor

with whom she could talk about all this, directly, without any false modesty, whereas it took me more than forty years of my life for the same thing to happen to me with my relatives, my family, and even then it was watered down.

I thought I needed to bring her some pictures of you, as a youngster. After all, fifty years later she may have forgotten you. But Violette immediately gives me a gift. Looking at me, I who have lost the image of my mother, she recognizes you instantly. My forehead and the shape of my eyes, no doubt.

I tell her a lot about our life. Violette already knew some elements of it from Hélène and Fanny, with whom she had never completely lost contact. She knew the main episodes, marriage, birth, divorce, remarriage, one more birth, death, living far away on the edge of the United States. I explain to her in detail the feelings that have worked away at me with a chisel for so long, that of having spent my childhood with a quasi-absent mother, someone three-quarters destroyed by her experience. Violette amazes me when she talks about you out loud: your gentleness, your kindness, of course, which everyone in my family always spoke about with devotion. Still, I think, you could also be sour, unfair, and surly. But Violette confirms it: you were gentle, good and serene. Even in Birkenau!

Inside, in the warmth, we spend several hours talking: me about my relationship with you, and my regret at having passed you by, and Violette about her return from deportation. She tries to explain to me how, at the end of the war and with the all daily hardships, many "normal" people, as in those who hadn't been through Birkenau, very quickly wanted to turn over the page, or even just ignore it altogether. To make me understand the silence, she tells me about a surprise party she was invited to, sometime after her return. Someone hearing her talk about her story squealed and asked her to be quiet: it was too depressing. 'At that point, I decided to shut my mouth', she tells me. But in the silence that was expected of her, she describes how it also gave her a kick up the backside, by forcing her not to drown in her memories and to look as resolutely as possible towards the future: the incomprehension of others in light of what couldn't be spoken, constituted a paradox for her of an unbearable injustice and the impetus to move forward.

I can't help it: when I tell her of my frustration, my sadness, my emptiness, it's with vehemence and almost anger. It's as if, through her, I was speaking to you and, in a way, to everyone around you.

Without any shame, I confide in Violette, who went through what you went through, how I resigned myself very early on to protect you, and not to ask for more than what you could grant me. I also confide in her that I very quickly gave up on you telling me something about this time, and how hard that resignation still is for me.

I now understand. You who had known extreme hunger, the kind people die from, who knew fear, suffering, and horror, could you, so soon afterwards, identify with my cries for "normal" hunger, or the fear of being alone in the dark, or waking up after a nightmare? No doubt you couldn't bear to anymore.

Reluctantly, I pity you. I pity us, and I'm ashamed of this pity.

Lille, 1 July 1943
Violette has been living in the suburbs of Lille for a few months. She first left Le Havre with her parents who, in order to escape the bombings of 1940, had moved to Paris where they were confronted with the first discriminatory measures against the Jews. She still has her mother's identity card, issued by the Pétainist authorities, a green card with the word "Jew" stamped in diagonally in red, as if to bar any particular sign of height, weight or hair colour. On the advice of an uncle, they had then secretly come to seek refuge in the Lille region. Without registering at the prefecture, they must use forged food stamps. There's also no possibility of her parents finding work and no opportunity for Violette to enrol in high school. They manage to live by drawing on their savings, then

by reselling the clothing coupons that her father had brought with him from his store in Le Havre.

On 1 July, she returns home to rue Cabanis, in Fives, after going to the cinema to see *Le Lit à colones* (The Four-poster), a film with Jean Marais, Fernand Ledoux and Odette Joyeux. Fifty years later, she still remembers it with amusement: the character played by Jean Marais is a musician in prison, whose work is stolen by the prison director. By the time the screening ends, it's 4 o'clock in the afternoon.

She comes back by tram. Arriving near her home, she sees the curtains of the neighbouring house moving, and a slight concern hits her, which then turns into panic. She rings the doorbell and two men in black leather coats and trilby hats come out of her house. She knows what this means and starts to run: her mother has also gone to the cinema in Fives, and is due to return soon. Violette understands that she mustn't fall into the trap. She wishes she could fly away, but she isn't fast enough and is quickly caught by the Gestapo. They are used to the chase.

Cornered by the bull mastiffs, she is brought home and watches helplessly as her mother is captured. At the Gestapo headquarters in Lille they find an aunt, who for a time had been seeing a rather suspicious man known to be a petty trafficker and collaborator. It's clear to Violette that the simultaneous arrests can mean only one thing: they have been betrayed.

A long time later, and without any particular remorse, Violette admits that the fierce desire to discover their whistle blower and kill him was part of what supported her throughout her deportation. 'When I'm in prison, bring me apples, not oranges', she often said to her friends, seeing herself as quite the rebel. But the individual in question would later be executed by the FFI (Forces françaises de l'Intérieur).[3]

---

3. The French Forces of the Interior (FFI) was a group of French resistance fighters in the later stages of the Second World War.

Father, mother and daughter are all locked in individual cells at a prison in Loos. What Violette doesn't know is that this is the last time she will have a space to herself for two years. The food is foul, the isolation scary. One absurd detail is that every day a newspaper is slipped under the door, just as if they were in a grand hotel. She reads it from the first to the last line, even the classifieds. Eight days later, the family is escorted to Saint-Gilles prison, Brussels. The food there is better and they can wave to each other during their daily walk. A dozen or so days later, they are all taken to Mechelen transit camp, the penultimate stage of a journey that will take them to the borders of Europe, to a place where, without them knowing it, a destination has already been planned and organized for them by the Nazis. Auschwitz.

Although French, and only deported from Belgium by some bureaucratic accident, many years later Violette will have the unpleasant surprise of seeing her name inscribed on the monument to the Belgian dead of those deported from Mechelen.

They are deported on 31 July 1943 in convoy number twenty-one, which arrives at Auschwitz in the mid-morning of 2 August. They travel in a sealed wagon car: it's hot, and the unhygienic conditions and overcrowding are unbearable. The only toilet bucket allocated to the people in the wagon will, naturally, quickly overflow. Trying to retain some form of dignity and, perhaps, while also beginning to adapt her body to the unimaginable conditions, throughout the journey she doesn't need to crouch in the mire.

Upon arrival, the designation of those who will be killed immediately takes place on the station platform. In a reflex that she herself describes as "boy scout", Violette doesn't climb into the waiting truck, believing instead that the older people or those more strained by the journey will need it instead. First she is separated from her father, then watches as her mother gets into the truck. This sorting operation between those deemed 'fit' or 'unfit' to live takes place in a cacophony of howls, the barking of guard dogs, and seemingly contradictory orders. Yet if someone approaches the truck and expresses the desire to climb on board to be with a loved one, none of the SS guards says anything, or shows any sign of wanting to stop them.

Along with the other women designated to enter the camp, she passes through the gate and walks the approximately 1.3 kilometres of *Lagerstrasse*, the road which crosses the camp, to arrive at the "sauna" of Camp B. Here, they are all entered in the camp's records, shaved, 'disinfected', and are, finally, entitled to a shower. They are then taken to be tattooed and are given items of clothing: breeches, a shirt, a dress with a large slash of red paint on the back, shoes in their (approximate) size, and a bowl.

Violette doesn't understand the purpose of the truck. Why do you need one to cover such a short distance from the ramp? She's never seen any concern for the comfort of Jews before, and it worries her. Consequently, ever since her arrival she speaks to any inmates who pass by. 'What happened to the men who were with us? Where did my mother go when she got on the truck?' They all give the same answer: they went to another camp, where the work will be less hard because they are older.

During the process of tattooing her registration number on her forearm, Violette approaches an *Aufseherin*, a female SS guard, and in her very scholarly German asks her the same question. No doubt in order to avoid panic – *deutsche Ordnung* – than out of humanitarian concerns, the SS guard confirms that they have been sent to another, more comfortable, camp for the elderly. The elderly? Her father is 43 years old and her mother only 40! The answer doesn't ease her concern. The experiences she and her family have been through in the past month, the way in which they were thrown out of the wagon upon arrival at Auschwitz, none of this prepares her to accept the idea that the Nazis might do something not necessarily "correct", but at the very least, a little less "inhuman".

She continues to ask the same question to all the inmates she meets, and gets the same answer: 'They're elsewhere, in another camp.' Speaking to one of those responsible for tattooing the newcomers, she changes her tactic: 'One of my friends got into the truck when we arrived; do you know what happened to her?' They show her the thick grey smoke coming out of the chimney which dominates the whole camp, over there, at the end and to the right of *Lagerstrasse.*

'She might be there, in that plume of smoke...'

Then the murders are described to her in detail: the fake cloakroom, the fake soap, the fake shower room, the gassing, and the crematorium, the brutality of the narrative accurately reflecting the violence of the act itself. Complete incomprehension followed by a dreadful feeling of annihilation seizes her. The word "Jewish" stamped in red on her mother's identity card, the arrests, the incarcerations, the humiliations they had endured for more than a month, they had all finally found their conclusion.

What had shown itself to be mass suffering inflicted gratuitously had therefore resulted in *this*. The insane sequence of events had found its logical coherence: the deportees aren't there to work, which everyone had tried to believe and reassure themselves with, until they arrived in this place. They are there to die. Devastated, Violette regrets not having climbed into the truck with her mother, and not having died as well so that she would no longer have these visions of murder, and the suffering that resonates within her. Several hours after her arrival, she has really only just now entered the Auschwitz universe.

*   *   *

All the new arrivals from the Mechelen convoy are held in quarantine. For six weeks they are piled up in Block 9, in Camp A, which has been designed for this purpose. The block's commander

(*Blockowa*), is a Slovak called Suzanne, better known as Szuszi. A ferocious character, after the war she would be found guilty of having killed around 100 people and consequently executed by the British at the same time as Josef Kramer, the camp commandant; Irma Griese, another female SS guard; and others. During the war, however, through promotion, intrigue, and the demonstration of her ability to be obeyed "without fail", she became a *Lagerälteste*, the *Kapo* in chief of Belsen. Learning that Violette speaks Hungarian, even though she came from Le Havre, she asks if she knows a certain Madame Simon, a cousin of hers, who turns out to have been Violette's mother's best friend.

Suffering from dysentery shortly after her arrival, and also to see something else and move around a little, Violette decides to make herself sick. Szuszi takes her to the *Revier* (infirmary), advising her not to linger there. During this period of "hospitalisation", 18-year-old Violette wakes up one day to find that her neighbour has died in her sleep. It's the first time she has seen a dead woman, but she is already unable to name the object lying next to her as a "corpse". Her knowledge of life in the camp is growing fast.

At the same time as learning the realities of the camp, she also starts to assimilate the minimalist vocabulary which circulates there, a brutal mixture of German and Polish. New arrivals continue to flood in, sturdy Dutch women, Greeks too, tanned, still beautiful and happy, despite a terrible journey through half of Europe and their final destination. Among them, there is an enormous "waste". In the camp's slang, it means that an unbelievable proportion of prisoners die during this period of quarantine, often from despair and dejection rather than deprivation or disease.

Although from France, Violette is isolated in the block, which is primarily populated by Belgian women. She knows no one. The fate of her parents, and the devastating grief, cuts her off from her comrades. There are eight or nine of them per bedstead. Being *koya* companions – the Polish term for the boards they sleep on

– will sometimes also mean the first possible stage of unfailing friendships for the survivors. The food, involving coloured water called "coffee", tea or *herbata* (herbal tea in Polish), a quarter of bread, 25 grams of margarine, a translucent soup, is insufficient from the very beginning. In Camp B, once the quarantine period has passed, they have *Zulage* (bonus) three times a week; a supplement of bread and a slice of sausage, *Leberwurst*, margarine or a filthy beet jam: it's vile but sweet, and therefore nourishing. Violette suffers from whitlow[4] on her finger. Someone had told her to urinate on it to disinfect it, but since then her arm has begun to swell and she now has a fever.

*   *   *

A few days after entering quarantine, a *Läuferin* (a messenger), comes to the Block: 'Are there any musicians among you?' Violette had heard, as had everyone else in the Block, the sounds of a bass drum in the morning and evening, without initially being able to identify where it came from or what it was for. Then she realized there was an orchestra.

She had played the violin for a few years: her mother had thought it could "come in useful", and her father had paid for lessons by making jackets for her violin teacher. She is not, by any means, a virtuoso, and hadn't really played the instrument for three years. Having heard the camp orchestra play during their morning outing, and again when the *Aussenkommandos* returned in the evening, the idea of taking part doesn't stay in her mind for long. She knows her limits, and thinks that among the thousands of women present in the camp there must be many who are musically superior to her, both technically and practically. Refusing to make a fool of

---

4. A painful infection caused by the herpes virus.

herself, which in retrospect seems strange considering her location, she doesn't attend.

However, after a few days she notices the comings and goings of two young girls from the Block, Hélène and Fanny. Hélène is very young: tall, a little wistful and distant, she is only 16 years old and her teenage face is round and smooth. Her large, clear blue eyes often seem to be looking elsewhere, while the ash-blonde stubble on her head is already starting to curl a little. Fanny, meanwhile, is the complete opposite of Hélène: a brunette with dark eyes, she is lively and flirtatious and has known Violette since the camp at Mechelen.

Violette walks up to Hélène. She has finally found someone to talk to. A sudden urge seizes her.

'I play the violin, too, but I haven't done so since the war started. Do you think I can give it a go?'

'Well you have to audition, but you've got nothing to lose. Why don't you volunteer tomorrow?'

Although still in shock over her mother's death, Violette decides to try her luck anyway.

* * *

At that time, the orchestra has two functions, which all the inmates know about. The first, "practical" function, is to pace the march of those leaving the camp in rows of five to work outside, then the same on their return in the evening. The SS soon realize that it's easier to count people who are walking in step. The orchestra, a *Kommando* like the others, is set up at the front, facing the SS guard post at the entrance to Camp A. It plays military marches, punctuated by the bass drum and cymbals as they hammer out the '*links, links, links UND links*' of the slave march.

The second function of the orchestra, which is quite a perversion of the first, is to offer relaxation for the SS by providing them with a sort of living "jukebox" entirely at their discretion. And so Mengele, Tauber, Kramer, Mandl the *Oberaufseherin* [chief overseer], or any of the other executioners can enter the orchestra's Block to ask for the programme, select two or three pieces of music, listen to it, and then head back for a little more slaughter before returning home. They can even imagine that they have their own personal musicians, just like the high Germanic lords of the Middle Ages whom they claim to invoke.

The orchestra is conducted by a young Polish woman, who has been appointed by the SS. She's a pianist of moderate ability called Zofia Tchaïkowska, whom the Nazis perhaps foolishly think has a familial, and therefore genetic, connection to that of Pyotr Ilyich, her Russian namesake. Extremely restless, nervous and talkative, she massacres Chopin with great energy on the piano at the orchestra's disposal, before it's eventually moved to the officers' mess.

* * *

Violette doesn't delude herself when she stands in front of Tchaïkowska. She's been away from music for a long time, never mind being in poor condition herself physically. After having flayed Massenet's *Meditation* from *Thaïs*, she's hardly surprised to hear that she doesn't get the part. The audition takes place in the dormitory-dining room of the Block, and she's able to see the living conditions offered to the musicians: a ration of bread of which the *Kapos* don't take their share, and a 50-litre *Kübel* (bucket) of soup for forty people, where this time there's an equal mix of liquid and solids so that the broth becomes noticeably more nourishing. One bed per person, a fleece blanket (*Steppdecke*) and – supreme luxury! – a sheet, comfortable clothes, tables with benches: it all looks almost normal in this otherwise generalized misery. During a visit to the Block, Anne-Lise, another inmate and a friend of Violette's, even remembers seeing an entirely pointless object: a vase on top of a cupboard!

Back in her Block in Camp A, Violette is still able to spend time with Hélène and Fanny, who have to go back there every evening to sleep, at least until their quarantine period is over. Their more presentable appearance – they're already enjoying some of the perks of being musicians, not the least of which includes a daily shower – is starting to clash with the other inmates.

In early September 1943, Hélène informs Violette that a new conductor has been appointed, and that she absolutely has to audition once more. Drawing on the experience of her first audition, Violette offers to play a gypsy-style tune from *Countess Maritza*,[5] which isn't too technically difficult and has quite a catchy meoldy. Before she plays properly, she asks if she's allowed half an hour to warm up her fingers by completing a few scales and practising excerpts of the music, hoping that this warm-up ritual would help convince the other musician that she has experience.

Alma Rosé, newly appointed to conduct the orchestra, listens to the piece: 'this isn't famous!' she says. Violette's face falls. She would have preferred not to try at all. Having seen the daily diet of the girls in the orchestra, she feels like her life at Auschwitz is a bit like Tantalus's torment,[6] and believes she has obviously failed again.

Alma seems to understand what's happening with Violette. Maybe she even credits her with a desire, a need, to make music. She can relate to that perfectly, because that's what also drives her. After thinking for a few seconds, she throws a lifeline to Violette and, without either of them knowing it, puts both of them on the road to survival: 'Never mind, I'll take you on a trial basis. Maybe it'll improve. You'll have another audition in eight days.'

---

5. An operetta in three acts by Hungarian composer Emmerich Kalman.
6. Tantalus is a figure from Greek mythology who was made to stand in a pool of water beneath a fruit tree with low branches, with the fruit constantly eluding his grasp, while the water always recedes before he can take a drink.

Just like Hélène and Fanny, every day Violette must now walk the few hundred metres separating Block 9 in Camp A from the orchestra's Block, which is almost at the end of *Lagerstrasse*, in Camp B. This *Lagerstrasse*, pounded daily by tens of thousands of shoes, is dusty and dry in the summer, but turns into a quagmire at the beginning of autumn before becoming an icy swamp in which your feet sink, where the wooden and canvas clogs remain frozen, and where every step requires an extra effort required from already exhausted bodies.

Four days after her conditional acceptance into the orchestra, Violette finds herself without shoes: they were stolen overnight, no doubt to serve as currency. She must now make the regular journey barefoot in the icy mud. Tchaïkowska, the *Blockowa*, and head of the orchestra's Block following Alma's arrival, intercepts her. Before entering, she orders Violette to wash her feet in a tub of cold water that the musicians use to wash the mud from their shoes. Violette complies but, overcome with despair, starts to cry.

The orchestra arrives after playing at the gate for the departing *Kommandos*. To Alma, at this moment Violette is the image of what they're all going through: shaved, emaciated, frozen, and in tears.

'Why are you crying?'

Violette explains the situation.

'Alright, I'll get you into the orchestra right away, let's see...'

In no time at all, she takes her to the clothing warehouse, gives her warm clothes, normal shoes, woollen socks, and the musicians' uniform: a navy blue pleated skirt, a white blouse, and a white cotton headscarf for her hair. This is also what Auschwitz is: you can have your shoes stolen – which can cause death in a matter of days – and then your life can be saved a moment later. Only luck is in charge.

Although she's given stockings, with nothing to keep them in place Violette is permanently pulling them up her legs, making her look like a clown. With the foolish obstinacy of a chief warrant officer, the *Stubendienst* (barrack orderly), the everlasting Maria Langenfeld, harasses her until she finds a system to hold up her stockings. A facial paralysis distorts her face and makes her perpetually bark when she speaks. Violette replaces the elastic in her knickers with string, and uses the elastic as makeshift suspenders. Now, she no longer clashes with the rest of the girls in the group.

*   *   *

Violette sits at the third violins' desk. Their role isn't too difficult: they only have to play the down beats on the waltzes and a few counter melodies to support the tunes played by the lead instruments. However, Alma is no less rigorous and demanding with them than she is with the others.

Yet this return to almost human living conditions isn't without harm for Violette. Naturally inclined to associate with the group of Francophones, Belgians, French and Greeks, she doesn't immediately manage to integrate with the other women, and the loss of her parents remains acute. Diving in, as it were, before her quarantine period had ended, an empty sort of time punctuated by meals and trips to the latrines twice a day, her suffering is still present but has made her numb to what is going on around her. Yet she is now expected to have 'normal' relationships in a place where no form of sensitivity exists anywhere, and so the suffering hits her hard again.

During her first ten days in the orchestra, Violette is lost. An increasingly high fever appears: the inflammation in her arm is very painful, swelling up like an egg, and the first signs of typhus appear. All the while she remains overwhelmed by the death of her mother. She's in pain, mournful, and whimpers. Everyone avoids her. Clearly, depression leading to collapse and death can be as contagious as typhus.

Ten days after joining the orchestra, Violette enters the *Revier*, the typhus and a very high fever having left her practically unconscious. The phlegmon on her arm is incised and a makeshift dressing of embossed paper, instead of cotton wool, is applied directly on the incision, with a loose bandage to hold it in place. After a few days the intolerable itching becomes worse and, no longer able to bear it, she tears off the bandage that is practically welded to her arm: there are lice in her wound. To top it off, after seeing her do this, the *Revier* doctor simply slaps her: her bandage won't be replaced for several days, thus emphasizing her helplessness.

Throughout these three weeks, Violette is almost comatose and eats nothing. Despite this, she passes a 'selection' and, even if her spirit is too weak to carry on, her vitality takes over. During the selections, Mengele, or another Nazi "doctor", diagnoses the hospitalized inmates in three seconds. Those who are considered too weak are taken to Block 25 in Camp A to be gassed in the next day or two, fully aware of the fate that awaits them, unlike the victims selected on arrival at the camp.

Violette passes this first selection, even though she can barely stand: with her ruined body, she can't do anything else. She only knows that if she's directed to the left, then it is death. In this case she'll have to take advantage of her status as a member of the orchestra, and try to pass the information on to Alma, who may be able to prevent her transfer to Block 25.

It's also during these first three weeks in the *Revier* that the Block leader asks her to find the words for the Rina Ketty song, *J'attendrai* (I will wait) which has become a worldwide hit. In return, she receives a ration of bread that she can't bear to touch, but which she proudly keeps at the foot of her bed. None of her fellow inmates comes to visit her at the *Revier*, which clearly shows the extent of her isolation.

She survives another selection, fully aware of what's at stake. She decides to apply the technique everyone uses: tighten the abdominal muscles, or what's left of them, stick out the buttocks, keep the head very straight and the neck arrogant: 'I'm clearly healthy, how can you possibly think otherwise?' They are the tragic models of a pitiful parade, where it isn't a parade you're "selected" for, but the slaughterhouse.

After six weeks she leaves the *Revier*; she weighs barely 38 kilos when fully dressed. The date of her release is symbolic: 4 November is her parents' wedding anniversary.

*   *   *

During her hospitalisation at the *Revier*, Violette has time to reflect and is now more or less able to understand the main rules of survival at the camp. It was a happy coincidence that she'd learned to play the violin rather than the piano, and it was an unlikely lottery that had already enabled her to survive until now. She now knows that brooding over anxieties and depression are the first steps to collapse. She sees the Muslims, these prostrate and objectified women whose will to live has abandoned them, and that even all feeling seems to have deserted. Some are slumped on the stove pipe which crosses the Block: they suffer third degree burns on their legs but no longer show the slightest reaction.

Violette has now realized that she has to fight like never before; not just anyhow, though, and certainly not by trampling anyone in her path. She knows that she must block out her imagination at all costs in order to distance herself as much as possible from the virtual certainty of her death. She dreams that she is being put in the truck to be taken to the gas chamber. In her dream she doesn't struggle, pray or scream, and hopes she'll be as calm as that in real life, if that's what's to happen to her. There's no alternative but to live, not from day to day, but from minute to minute. The tattooing, the humiliations, the beatings, you survive it. Only death is final.

Back from the *Revier*, she goes to visit a friend in an ordinary Block and sees a silhouette in front of her. She wonders who it could be, only to realize that it's her reflection in the window. She didn't even recognize herself. She borrows a cardboard box, a blanket and a knife (used to cut the bread into thin slices and to spread the margarine) from one of the girls, Génia, who was at *Revier* at the same time as her. Génia plays the mandolin and the two women have bonded. However, the loan is frowned upon by everyone, and it even seems to be worse than if she'd stolen it: isn't that a way of saying Génia will never come back from the hospital? Violette says that she will, of course, return everything to its owner upon her return, but Génia dies of typhus and so never comes back to the Block. Violette's integration into the orchestra continues to be difficult.

* * *

Shortly after returning to the Block, Violette is assigned a new role. The members of the orchestra sit on wooden stools, their music stands in front of them. Meanwhile, Alma stands on a podium, alone. Yet all this paraphernalia needs to be carried every day from the Block to the place where they play, in front of the gates to Camp A. The stands are heavy and made of wood, and Violette is still very weak.

Cursing the whole world, and Alma in particular, she carries her load. Limping and breathless, she's quickly left behind by the others and passes in front of Franz Hössler, the camp commandant before Josef Kramer. One of the basic rules of survival in the camp is not to stand out from the mass of inmates. But Violette's thinness and weakness are hard to ignore.

'Who is this Muslim girl?' Hössler asks Alma. Violette's life is now in danger.

'One of my best violinists,' replies Alma, saving her life for the second time.

'In which case, you'd better build her up a bit; put her on the diet for three months.'

The "diet" is a mark of favour: an extra litre of soup, sweet oatmeal porridge, and white bread. The extra rations allow you to exchange the surplus for something else, such as soap, a knife, a favour etc. Violette is a triple winner: she's avoided a third 'selection' and is now being given extra food. When she arrives back at the Block, the inmates who had witnessed the exchange between Alma and Hössler from afar question her and show their concern. Now she's part of a group, her chances of survival have further improved without her really knowing it. She is now, finally, fully integrated into the orchestra.

Chapter 2

An Anniversary

Brussels, 15 April 1995

We meet at Hélène's large house in Brussels, four generations together, accompanied by Anita Lasker, who has come from London, Éva Steiner, from Munich, Hélène's mother, her daughter, grandson, and other members of her family. Violette's two children are there, along with Louis, Fanny's husband, in order to celebrate the fiftieth anniversary of their liberation from Belsen on 15 April 1945, the day after your twenty-second birthday.

This isn't the first time the anniversary on 15 April has been celebrated. Violette had told me about it. Violette, Hélène, Anita and Fanny, who have now disappeared, had been meeting for about fifteen years. These encounters were times for remembering, but not mourning, because crying or feeling sorry for themselves wasn't their style.

They would go out together, to restaurants or to the theatre; they once went to a concert to listen to Anita play the cello in the English Chamber Orchestra. They would smile or burst out laughing. However, there always came a moment in these encounters, when memories arose, where they evoked the dead and the living, those who had disappeared in the camps, as well as those who had died afterwards. They had forged a relationship in that place that nothing would dissolve, the strength of which was felt from the outside, and these meetings on 15 April nurtured that link, as well as reaffirming its significance. Even Fanny's death hadn't prevented these meetings from continuing.

Hélène thought that this fiftieth anniversary celebration, organized in Brussels, should also be shared, particularly by those of the generations that came after. We watch Violette arrive with a Hungarian cake made from chocolate and nuts. She had promised Hélène fifty years earlier that if they survived Auschwitz she would make it for her one day. On the top of the cake, Violette has written "50" in almonds.

We are also able to see the reunion of Violette and Éva, who haven't seen each other since 1945. Even though it takes place in Hungarian, their mother tongue, it's a moving exchange for us to witness from the outside.

*　*　*

The contrast between the women is very stark. Anita, tall, strong, with fairly short cropped silver hair, and a surprisingly smooth forehead and deep eyes, speaks plainly, without any flourishes. When I meet her for the first time, I have the feeling I know her already, as Violette has told me all about her. I'm a little light-headed when I see her, almost ready to burst. When she speaks French, her German accent makes her diction faster, colder, more distant than she would probably like. Her firm handshake seems to tell me: 'You keep your distance and pull yourself together, we don't give in to any sweet sentimentality!'

Éva is a bit more distanced. Her exquisitely delicate body and features immediately remind me of a porcelain doll, fragile and precious. She is stronger than that though: she survived, and continued to live on afterwards. She was a singer, and her voice still modulates a little when she speaks. Her accent is Eastern European, and softens an otherwise somewhat shrill voice. She has trouble remembering you, and even now gives me the impression that she's trying to shield herself from the visions and nightmares by putting aside the painful memories. She can't remember the songs she used to sing there. Strangely, when she speaks of Maria Mandl, SS chief overseer of the women's camp, she calls her 'Frau Mandl', as if the submission required in the relationship between inmates and SS guards has resurfaced without warning.

I hug Hélène very closely, for her, for you, for me. I'm here to represent you, yet for all that we aren't going to talk about you very much, because this party is all about luck and life. Louis, Fanny's husband, can't place me very well; am I Elsa's brother, or her husband? No, her only son.

This year the anniversary meal coincides with that of Passover, the commemoration of the exodus from Egypt. However, I find it hard to see what you went through as a test sent by a compassionate god. The parallel with your liberation from Belsen by the English armoured divisions doesn't seem particularly relevant to me. I find it even more difficult to see the hand of God, or even a reincarnation of Moses, in the person of Field Marshall Bernard Montgomery, the hero of El Alamein. Éva is at the end of the table, far away. Anita smokes continuously for some of the ceremony, then dozes a little. Violette sighs. She's extremely bored and fidgets a little in her chair. Hélène, who's placed me on her left, appears to be happy. She smiles. She must be thinking of you. I think about you, too. We're able to talk to each other once the ceremony is over. I'm often silent and look at the four of them, moved and fascinated. Olivier, Violette's son, is upset and doesn't want to miss out on anything.

*   *   *

The idea of preserving your story, in any way possible, definitely occurred to me at this point. The bond between you, Hélène and Fanny was so strong that nothing could have penetrated it, and I have neither the desire nor the ability to work it out. It consisted of experiences so far beyond my comprehension that it would be absurd even to try. Although I felt excluded from it, I'm deeply happy – for you and for the others – that it was able to exist and keep going. I no longer feel the anger or frustration I used to feel when our family worshipped you.

A similar bond exists between Hélène, Violette and Anita. The strength of this bond is almost palpable and they agree to talk about what holds it together. Through their experiences, I might come across something about you that escaped me during your lifetime, and from which your death almost cut me off: the echo of your emotions and your pain of this moment in history.

Finally, the women in this orchestra, the people who'd been through what you went through, accept my requests to know you through your experiences, and from which you always kept me away. At last, I can put away this lingering feeling of breaking into a story that doesn't belong to me, where I don't belong myself, whose characters are supposed to have been so degraded from what they'd endured that it's better to leave it all buried.

Before she takes the train back to London, I have a conversation with Anita. She thinks she knows what I want; for her to talk to me about you. She asks me in particular what it is that's been missing for us, those who came "afterwards", since we had no war and deprivation to prevent us from living. I confess to her how much the silence about your past was painful to me. She understands straight away, because it confirms what she's already heard. I ask her the question that has haunted me since my meeting with Violette. I've always been told about my gentle and serene mother, who was incapable of being vindictive. No doubt she had arrived there like that, domesticated and submissive after twenty years of a difficult family life. I, who had known you in another context, could attest to this: you were unable to fight for yourself, whatever the outcome. But how can one have been gentle and serene in Birkenau and have survived?

Anita answered me. A key to your survival may have been simple luck, which you didn't have much of afterwards. Another factor must have been Dora, a 14-year-old girl you tried to protect.

Dora... I'd heard that name before in my family, when I didn't have to listen to what the grown-ups were saying. I imagine a child, and you, careful to do whatever you could to protect her: a caress, a smile, a little bit of hope, a piece of bread or soap... Two trapped birds leaning on each other. I see you, willing to offer yourself as a sacrifice in her place, as you've always known how to do.

I understand that your famous sense of responsibility kept you from letting go, whenever someone else was involved. A vague and absurd jealousy takes hold of me. Had Dora exhausted your ability to pay attention to me over time, just a few years later? I see you in Birkenau protecting this child. The images swarm in my head and the rest of your life with me is as if you'd stayed there, leaving me with a father so absent that he was almost abstract.

I think back to a piece of paper I found at my sister's house, indicating the date of your deportation from Mechelen transit camp: convoy No. 20, 19 April 1943, five days after your twentieth birthday. I feel sorry for you and in a flash, for the second time in my life, I see you there, you and Dora, whom I've never seen before.

Birkenau, April 1943

As soon as she arrives in Birkenau, Elsa can feel it in her bones: death is everywhere. As she jumps out of the wagon she has to start unlearning what she's always considered to be the only acceptable attitude: politeness, understated elegance and self-effacement – some members of her family even called it submission. On the ramp she sees the way in which the weakest, the less agile, the most fragile, the old, the sick, and the children are treated; traits and individuals she has always learned to respect. In a deafening noise the blows fall like hail, the howls and barks propel them forward, as the ranks begin to form. Now the separation into two groups takes place; men on one side, women and children on the other. The noise now is even more trying, the calls from one group to the other, from a husband to his wife, from children to their father or mother.

Nothing and no one could have prepared Elsa for this infinite suffering, this insane directive that's now taking hold. While the Nazis organize this compact mass of people with blows from their truncheons, a swarm of skeletons dressed in striped outfits rush into the wagons to remove the thousands of packages and suitcases from the deportees, then set about cleaning the floor of the wagons with great jets of water.

The two groups begin to move off, marching towards the front of the train. A few trucks are waiting on the right-hand side. People are boarding fairly slowly there, but they aren't being beaten.

Everything moves pretty quickly from this point on. In no time at all, Elsa finds herself in front of an SS officer, who sends her to the left with a nonchalant gesture of his whip. There's a group of women there, for the most part young. There are no children and no elderly women. Obviously, she was chosen for something specific. But why this choice in such a short space of time?

The revelation by another, older inmate soon after entering the camp of what has happened to those not chosen alongside her, puts Elsa on the verge of collapse. She now knows where that greyish smoke comes from, the stench of flesh and burned fat that penetrates everywhere and permeates their clothes, the bricks of the Quarantine Block where she was thrown with the others, and even the earth, this Auschwitz earth, beaten, trampled and trodden by thousands of shoes from thousands of women who tramp over it all day long.

* * *

Elsa arrives at Auschwitz on 22 April, shortly after her twentieth birthday, which she hadn't celebrated in Mechelen. It'd been a long time since her family, her broken family, had wished her a happy birthday anyway, as the opportunities for celebration were severely limited. She'd had to stop her studies, however promising, because she needed to work in order to help her father, a leatherworker, to make luxury handbags and belts. Opportunities for laughter were rare. A vague nostalgia carries her through, but not for too long as it hurts to think of real life, on the other side of the barbed wire. At 20 she could've done so many unimportant and yet essential things to celebrate the occasion: go to the movies, listen to music, go dancing… Instead, she finds herself shaved, branded like an animal, clad in rags, and trapped in a place straight out of a nightmare. This place is simply unimaginable. She's fallen into this Birkenau world, whose boundaries are merely barbed wire.

It is in quarantine that she thinks she can distinguish musical notes, often hesitant, and not always *a tempo*, but overall something like Schubert's *Military March*. Twice a day she distinctly hears this music, in the morning around 6 o'clock, and again in the evening around 7 o'clock. She no longer has a watch, but feels that it is regular, if not regulatory. In the hubbub of the camp, and that of the Block where she's locked up for twenty-three hours a day, the wind occasionally brings her a few scattered notes. She can hear a flute, and even an accordion.

In this otherworldly context, the music appears as an additional strangeness or perversion. Yet Elsa has more to worry about than finding out where it comes from; staying alive even for a short time already seems like a tremendous task.

For the first time in her life, Elsa tells herself she needs to react. Her natural tendency would usually be to let herself sink in, to die in silence, like the two, three or ten women they find dead in their beds the following morning. She watches as inmates throw themselves onto the electrified barbed wire and die in a shower of sparks, or walk slowly through the forbidden zone, a few metres before the fence, where anyone who ventures is immediately shot by the guards from the top of the watchtowers. The thought of doing the same crosses her mind.

She doesn't know what happened to her father, who was arrested at the same time as her, let alone what will happen to her three brothers, who are hidden somewhere around Brussels. The combination of anguish and uncertainty for the lives of others is a very heavy load to bear for a 20-year-old girl.

But then there's Dora, and that changes everything.

Dora had lived with her parents and sister on the first floor of a house in Waterloo, the same house where Elsa's family had occupied the ground floor, and had had a bit of a crush on Louis, one of Elsa's brothers. Much later, Elsa learns that Louis had wandered all night following their arrest by the Gestapo; chivalrous and ridiculous, for hours he'd even wondered whether offering himself in exchange would give Elsa a chance of being released by the Nazis.

Elsa feels strangely guilty about Dora. After their arrest, she and Dora were taken together in a civilian bus to the Gestapo headquarters in Brussels, where they were guarded by Belgian gendarmes or somewhat ferocious German soldiers. Dora had wanted to escape but, as usual, Elsa was too afraid.

Ever since then she's felt responsible for the child. Dora doesn't stop crying. She's afraid of everything and everyone, and snuggles up against her. Elsa, who isn't exactly very strong either, pretends to be calm and confident about the future in order to reassure Dora. But now she'll do for the other girl what she thought she could never do before: she'll try to fight for survival. Try to fight against a world under constant pressure. To fight against despair in the face of the everyday inhumanity in front of her, and to fight against this tendency into submission that has shaped her entire life as a child, and then as a teenager.

*   *   *

I learned recently that you were probably reported by the people who owned the house. Your lack of malice and your innocence meant that throughout your detention, you never wondered to whom you owed your betrayal.

When, shortly after their arrival, a *Läuferin* enters the Block to ask if there are any musicians, the idea of exploiting the few years of studying the violin she did a long time ago doesn't occur to Elsa. Typical. She probably didn't feel up to it anyway. Another inmate, Bertha, a distant cousin that she'd found in the camp, pushes her forward for it.

She follows the *Läuferin* across Camp A, the quarantine camp, to the guard post, then the no man's land separating Camp A from Camp B, and finds herself in a wooden Block, far too close to the chimneys and their constant smoke: the transports are arriving from all over Europe these days.

Upon entering, she falls into another world. There's no screaming, nor that general atmosphere of self-abandonment that dominates the other camp. The Block is still under construction and follows the standard model of the other wooden Blocks, those that make up the part to the right of the *Lagerstrasse* of the women's camp: two rooms, separated by a wooden partition.

In the first room she's amazed to see a dozen women playing a military march as best they can, with a thoroughly assorted collection of instruments. The atmosphere is almost studious; the brick stove is almost hot.

There are two accordions, three clarinets, a flute, a cello, two violins, guitars, mandolins… In a corner of the main hall, not far from the cubicle which serves as a bedroom for the *Blockowa*, a table is set up for the *Schreiberinen*, the copyists who transcribe the conductor's' arrangement ideas onto manuscript paper.

None of it sounds very good, but at least now she understands the origin of the music she's heard morning and evening since arriving at the camp. Her astonishment turns to panic when a tall, strong woman asks her, in Polish-accented German, what instrument she plays and for how long, before putting a violin and a sheet of music in her hands.

Even with the little experience she's already gained in this unlikely world, Elsa clearly still has a lot to learn. You must pass an audition at Auschwitz, that's why she's here. Rather laboriously, she starts to play the score in front of the other women, and in front of the great Polish lady, Sofia Tchaïkowska. With what little esteem she has in her abilities, Elsa is sure to fail.

Either out of compassion, or because she's not very musical, or, quite simply, because she can't afford to be too selective, Tchaïkowska doesn't seem unhappy with what she hears: 'Well, I'll take you. You must come here every day to work on the repertoire, but you'll have to wait until the end of your quarantine before you can live here. Now, go rejoin the others.'

*   *   *

The others. There are two Greek accordionists: Yvette Assael, and Lily, her sister. They are complete opposites: Lily is small, round, stocky. She seems strong and self-assured, and constantly taunts her younger sister, who's about ten years her junior. Her anger and rants aren't always tolerated very well by the group. Yvette, meanwhile, is shy and casts a vaguely knowing smile towards the new girl. She's very young, barely 15, dark-haired, thin, and even the striped uniform fails to make her look ugly.

Hilde Grünbaum, a violinist, is a young, dark-haired German Jew who's brave and determined. Elsa will join her: Hilde witnessed the destruction of her own family and didn't fall apart. She'd been a member of a Zionist organisation for several years and had first discussed with her comrades whether or not she should join the orchestra. She had the good musical training, including music theory, harmony and violin that was given to any young German girl from a 'good family', at least until Nazism arose to define what a "good family" meant. Theoretically she could join the orchestra without too much difficulty. Nevertheless, it was a matter of conscience: wasn't voluntarily entering into a Nazi project a form of collaboration? However, it was decided that not only should she join the new orchestra, but she would also do everything she could to ensure that all her comrades in the organisation who had the slightest musical ability were quickly integrated into it as well. Hilde would be the first Jew to join.

Other members of the same organisation had arrived in the same convoy as Hilde: Ruth Bassin, Sylvia Wagenberg and her older sister, Carla, can play a bit of *Blockflöte* (recorder), as can all children who attended German schools. More importantly, however, they can read music and so were immediately accepted into the orchestra. Like Lily, Carla also often criticizes her younger sister.

Next to them is Mrs Kroner, the leader. Everyone calls her "auntie" or Frau Kroner, out of respect, including Tchaïkowska. Yvette, the youngest, believes she must be about 90 years old because she seems so old in comparison to her. "Auntie", a professional musician before the war, had played the flute in a philharmonic orchestra. Her sister Maria, a cellist, soon begins to complain of headaches and of feeling very weak. It's the first signs of typhus, from which she dies soon afterwards.

There are several quasi-violinists, mostly Polish women, the two Henrykas, and Maria. There are mandolin and guitar players and, finally, some Poles and two Ukrainians, Bronia and Szura. There are only a dozen women in all, but it's already a veritable Babel tower of languages. Lily and Yvette speak or chat to each other in Greek, Hilde, Sylvia, Carla, Ruth and the Kroner sisters speak in German, while Bronia and Szura, the guitarists, manage to chat with the Poles in Russian.

The whole group will communicate – with difficulty – in the appalling language of the camps, which is German, but strongly coloured with Polish and Russian. For example, the women responsible for the upkeep of the barracks, the military alignment of the mattresses and, above all, the distribution of food, have a functional name given to them by the Nazis: they are the *Stubendienst*. In the Polish camps they will be called *Stubowa*, a clumsy Polonisation of the German word, but less time-consuming. Similarly, Tchaïkowska, the *Blockälteste* (literally the block elder, or leader) of the orchestra's Block will be referred to as *Blockowa*.

Elsa was born in Germany, but had left in 1933 at the age of 10 because her parents were undoubtedly more aware of the growth of Nazism than others at the time. She was a refugee with her family first in France, then in Belgium, and already has a long history of drifting. However, she's fluent in Yiddish, German and French, and will serve as both a translator and as a bridge between the group – the clique – of Germans, French-speaking Greeks, French and Belgians.

Elsa hates conflict, having seen too much of it in her own family. Right until the end she'll often try to smooth things over, to erase those disagreements that are inevitable in a community, and to dispel any linguistic misunderstandings. However, this role as a musician means she'll also be able to protect Dora a little better.

Dora can often be found waiting in front of the Block's door. Terrorized by the great Polish *Blockowa* of the orchestra, she doesn't dare enter and prefers instead to wait for Elsa to come out to see her. Aware of the calmer atmosphere of the orchestra Block, she's there as often as possible. Fifty years later, she'll tell me that she would hide there, under Elsa's bed, during the camp "selections". Elsa reassures her with her quiet manner: she's always even-tempered, never speaks harshly to the young girl, and gives her what she can to help her survive, be it bread, warm clothes or just a kiss good night.

Later, perhaps with help from Elsa, Dora will manage to enter *Kanada*, the *Kommando* for sorting through the clothes of new arrivals at Auschwitz.

Chapter 3

The Chaconne[7]

Brussels, 16 April 1995

After having accompanied Éva back to the Brussels-South railway station, Hélène takes me to see my uncle, your brother Louis. Along the way, we talk about music. I go first. I like rock, pure, hard rock. Then she begins to tell me about her own music, her story, and her *Chaconne* in particular.

She hasn't seen Louis for over thirty years, long before your death. At my invitation, she speaks about the *Chaconne* again. Louis picks up his guitar and starts playing. It's difficult: there are wrong notes, and the guitar he's using is a poor instrument. However, Hélène visibly relaxes and smiles as she listens to the music. Are her beautiful blue eyes even brighter than usual?

I knew from childhood that this tune was special to you, that it had a deep meaning and a hidden value. I was once again in solidarity with you and could understand things about you that were previously incomprehensible to me. For you the *Chaconne* was Birkenau, that was irreparable, but it was also the arrival of Hélène into your life, and a truly decisive act on your part that had helped someone to survive. You didn't have a recording of the violin playing the piece, but you did have the guitar version, played by Andrés Segovia, which I'd already listened to at your house in Cologne. It was one of the discs I wasn't allowed to touch

---

7. A Chaconne is an example of musical composition, typical of the Baroque era, and takes the form of a continuous variation, typically characterised by a short, repeating bass line or harmonic progression.

and which only you could put on the turntable. Was that to avoid scratching it, or risking finding me alone with your visions?

For me, and for Louis, this *Chaconne* that we know by heart will never have the same meaning again. Until our final days we'll still see Hélène, that child, standing in front of these astonished women, in tears, in hell, surrounded by madness and murder.

Afterwards, my uncle will tell me how sometimes waves of uncontrollable emotions surface when he plays this piece, even to the point where he has to stop playing. I've often told this story to relatives or strangers, and I still struggle to remain calm whenever I bring it up. Hélène and her violin, an artist in the abyss, in a little moment of light and a few minutes of quiet heroism. A few free musical notes, no military marches, just music, which perhaps for a few minutes took you away and put you back in the realms of humanity for a short while. You were a number, a Birkenau shadow, who didn't cry, but survived, and then later burst into tears. Those tears were your return to humanity, because you cried as well, didn't you?

Brussels, June 1943

Hélène and her brother, Léon, five years her junior, are living in Brussels. Their parents, who arrived from Poland in 1928 when Hélène was a year old, have been hiding in a cellar since the Nazis invaded Belgium and the anti-Jewish measures were enforced shortly after. Her father is a cabinetmaker and her mother polishes the wood: they manage to survive by making polished mahogany animals that a Belgian businessman later sells on the market.

Hélène is a musician at heart. As soon as she heard her first piece of music for the violin – Bach's *Violin Partita* – she understood that this was her calling and managed to persuade her father to buy her a second-hand violin. Second-hand, but still expensive for a relatively poor family where even the smallest purchase required sacrifice. Yet Hélène will still have her violin, and will start learning to play it at 11 years old. By the standards of the time it's already a late age to start learning a new instrument, but she's a gifted student and progresses quickly, attending the Saint-Gilles Academy, practising at home, and entering the Conservatory.

Very early on, and with the temerity of her young age, she set off on her own – without really having the necessary technique – in the study of Bach's *Sonatas*. However, she still works on shorter classical pieces with her teacher, including Beethoven's *Romances* in A and in F. Her parents support her in their own way: her mother is proud and approves of her unconditionally, her father listens to her play while he works, and picks her up when she stumbles on a difficult section and repeats it over and over again: 'You're always scratching away at that violin. When are you going to play a whole piece?'

She studies the 'Ševčík' method, used in all Russian academies. It's a concentration of all the technical difficulties of the violin and once mastered, the student also masters their instrument. Hélène can't wait to start working on the piece that initially motivated her to start learning, the one she fell in love with: the *Chaconne*, the 3rd movement from Bach's *Partita in D minor* for solo violin. The work is a monument, with dozens of variations on an initial theme. The difficulty of it makes people shudder and causes more than one give up. When she feels ready, she works on it tirelessly, until exhaustion, and learns it almost clandestinely. Her teachers at the Conservatory ignore her; no doubt they would have screamed if they had known what she was daring to try.

Faced with Nazi persecution, her parents seek a way to make their children safe, but the choices are limited. One option is to hide them in Catholic institutions, with the fear of seeing them be converted and deny them their culture. One of Hélène's music theory teachers suggests they place the children in one such establishment. The alternative would be for Hélène to enter into an arranged marriage, aged just 14, with an older classmate from the Conservatory.

Everything seems to point in favour of the second solution. The marriage would automatically give Hélène Belgian nationality, which should keep her safe. Moreover, it was agreed with the future husband and his parents that the union would be dissolved as soon as the danger was over. Given Hélène's young age, special dispensation is requested from the rabbi and the future spouses queue for hours at the town hall to obtain the necessary papers for their marriage and naturalisation. Unfortunately, the illusion that Belgian nationality would give Jews protection against the Nazis is widespread, but it will make no difference.

The promise to dissolve the marriage is signed, and the document hidden in a hollowed-out chair. In return for a pension, Léon and Hélène will go to live with the family of the "husband" to await the end of the war and the persecutions.

*   *   *

In the early morning of 15 June 1943, three men in civilian clothes burst into the apartment. Hélène and Léon have been denounced. They're first taken to the Gestapo headquarters on Avenue Louise, where Hélène will be interrogated, then transferred directly to the transit camp in Mechelen. The camp is located in an abandoned barracks where future deportees are locked up, awaiting departure to what are supposed to be labour camps, somewhere in the east. Speculation is rife in the dormitories where families are gathered, and between the bunk beds, ideas on where people will be sent and what work they'll be forced to do are exchanged. The main thing is not to be separated. The general living conditions and food are acceptable and life in the camp is well-organized: there are tailors and hairdressers. Hélène and Léon are locked up, but they're together. As for the rest, the hope is to survive Hitler. The unimaginable has no place, because there is no need to go there.

In the camp, Hélène will meet a young girl who was arrested before her, Fanny Kornblum. They're introduced to each other, because propriety is still respected, despite the promiscuity and internment.

Shortly after their arrival in Mechelen, Léon is diagnosed with Furunculosis (an infection of the hair follicle), which requires hospitalisation: he is treated before being sent to die. Hélène will never see him again. When they are deported in convoy No. 21 on 31 July 1943, they are in two separate wagons. Hélène is in a "normal" wagon, that is to say a cattle wagon, the floor of which is strewn with straw, while Léon will travel east in a "medical car", whose occupants will all be gassed upon arrival – including those nurses who refused to abandon their patients.

The journey is eventful. The whole wagon is made up of young, courageous and determined people, who know that prisoners from the previous convoy managed to escape along the way. After refusing to go to what they still believe will be a labour camp somewhere in Germany, they equip themselves with tools stolen from the Mechelen camp, including saws, hammers and screwdrivers, and decide to try their luck as well. They saw a wooden rectangle into the floor of the wagon, and a few decide to risk it. However, warned of potential escapees, the Nazis reinforce the *Schutzpolizei* – the over-equipped and trained assault police in charge of guarding the train – and the young people who try to escape are all shot. One of them is found a short time later; after being shot in the abdomen, he'd travelled several kilometres in the night, holding his stomach, trying to find help before dying, emptied of his blood.

* * *

They arrive at Auschwitz on 2 August 1943. It's mid-morning, and they immediately fall into this unimaginable universe. The wagon doors open with a nightmare crash as the SS yell 'Raus,

Schnell!' and bludgeon the deportees who are too slow to descend onto the "ramp"; a simple earth embankment raised along the track to roughly the level of the camp's main gate, a few hundred metres further on.

The arrival takes place amid a chorus of screaming and barking, and a commotion of inmates dressed in striped uniforms; live skeletons scrambling all over the place. They empty the wagons of soiled straw, as well as the luggage belonging to the arrivals. All this while running like mad in all directions. An indescribable smell of burnt and rotting flesh hits them like a punch to the stomach. Hélène, who has never witnessed someone die, guesses that this is the smell of death, a horrifying death.

The new arrivals are separated; men on one side, women and children on the other, all adding to the confusion. People call each other from one line to the next, screaming at the top of their lungs to be heard. Everyone is lined up, beaten into place with sticks, and in paroxysms of howling. The "selection" is made as people stand in front of an indifferent SS officer who waves his whip, pointing behind him either left or right. The left is towards the camp, the right is towards the trucks waiting along the railway tracks.

This universe is obviously one where Hélène isn't thrown into to work, but to be killed: the Nazis don't even ask her what her profession is before directing her towards the entrance of the camp. With the rest of the "selected", she passes under a brick archway; an opening in a large building almost a kilometre in length, surmounted by a pointed tower. Up close it looks like a gigantic caricature of a head, the mouth of which is the main entrance, with its two malicious eyes being the windows above. They pass under this incredible gateway and turn to the left, to the women's camp.

Hélène is unable to stop crying, still unaware, at this point, that it's purely a biological chance that she hasn't been gassed upon arrival: children don't enter the camp, but are killed immediately. However, Hélène is tall for her age and her body is no longer quite that of a teenager. Despite her smooth, round face and childish features, her big blue eyes blink in disbelief as she becomes delusional.

For Hélène, the whole process takes place in a fog. Like the rest of her comrades, she will first be sheared and shaved; seeing her ash-blonde hair, still wavy, mingling with others on the floor in the Block where the operation is taking place makes her feel utterly helpless and unreal. In the full sense of the word, this place can't be possible. As a final humiliation, a number, 51887, is tattooed on her left arm. She's marked as an animal for slaughter. She'll quickly have to learn to remember this number at all times, particularly in German. Her name is no longer Hélène Wiernik, but 51887, 'Ein und fünfzig acht hundert sieben und achtzig'.

She's given a tattered dress, a few rags, a bowl and a spoon, before being taken with her comrades to the quarantine block, Block 9, where the new arrivals are confined. It's a stone building in Camp A, just a few steps away from Block 10, where Dr Mengele conducts his medical experiments on human guinea pigs.

Nine or ten women are crammed into each bed, sleeping on the planks with only a single thin blanket, no matter the weather. They remain locked up, lying on the dirt floor all day long. There's nothing to drink but polluted water. Ironically, the Nazi guards post a sign saying 'kein trinkbar Wasser' (not drinking water), as if they were concerned about the health of those daring or suicidal enough to drink it... Indeed, the water contains a great deal of iron oxides and carries one of the two forms of typhus that the prisoners catch in Birkenau. The other, Flecktyphus, is transmitted by lice. In quarantine, many people die.

* * *

In this atmosphere of devastation, the 16-year-old Hélène is unable to fight back. She keeps telling herself that she's in a nightmare and soon starts to break down. A neighbour, touched by her despair, tries to calm her down. 'If you're asked what your profession is, tell them you're a seamstress.'

'But I don't even know how to sew!'

'Don't worry, I'll teach you.'

Slumped on the ground in front of the Block, Hélène continues to cry. Then a thought comes to her, and doesn't go away: 'I'll never be able to play the violin again!' She begins to pace around in the tight space, injuring herself on the rough edges and pebbles on the ground, all the time thinking about her violin. It's a childish thought, and a ridiculous and absurd one in such a place. At the same time, it's a child's farewell, as well as that of an artist to life and to human civilization. A civilization so far out there, in time and space, and one that didn't desire her death.

As she describes it to me, it was precisely when she thought she was no longer playing – no longer living – that the miracle happened. As she says: 'an angel came down from heaven'.

A well-groomed, "civilized" young girl with a white kerchief on her head, dressed in normal clothes with lace-up, comfortable shoes, walks towards her after speaking with a group of women from the Block. Is she a Nazi? Or a warden?

She addresses Hélène in French: 'Apparently you play the violin?'

Hélène is stunned. Can you talk about music here? She's lost everything, and now knows that she's in a place that was meant to be the death of her and her people. They told her about the fate that awaited those on the ramp who were designated for the trucks. She knows where the smell that seized her came from as soon as she arrived, she knows how the smoke and flames from the tall chimneys far back behind Camp B are produced. The mention of the violin, evoking her life "before", comes like an echo to answer the question that torments her, and makes her suffering even more acute, her awareness of the irreparable.

The young woman in the white kerchief had learned that a transport had arrived from Mechelen, and wanted a musician, whoever she might be, from the Block. Miraculous news – an inmate told her there was a violinist among the new arrivals.

'Yes, I can play.'

'For how long?'

'Five years.'

'They all say that. But if it's true, you come with me.'

Still in shock, Hélène rebels and responds in a muffled rage: 'I really have been playing for five years. But there's no way I'm playing to distract the Germans!' The woman insists, 'Shut up and follow me.'

Her companion, the seamstress, encourages her. Hélène will later try to find this first friend to bring her something to eat, only to learn that she hadn't survived quarantine: typhus.

Hélène finally agrees and follows the woman who came to get her. She leads her to Camp B, where the orchestra's Block is, and where she'd already been a short time earlier to be shaved. The Block is at the very end, the penultimate one on the right of *Lagerstrasse*. At the far end, the large chimneys spew swirls of grey, oily smoke, ashes and soot over the whole camp, adding a further stench to the ambient pestilence.

The few hundred metres they have to cover are painful for Hélène: she walks barefoot and injures herself on the gravel path of the *Lagerstrasse*, the road lined with rows of barracks up to the electrified barbed wire of the compound, and which crosses the camp to lead, beyond the barbed perimeter, to what she learned was the gas chamber and crematorium No. II. While the buildings on the left are made of stone, those on the right are made of wood.

She hasn't been given any shoes because in the quarantine Block, a large proportion of inmates are condemned to die from typhus, dysentery, or simply from despair. As far as those running the Nazi camp are concerned, donating shoes only to have them recovered from corpses a few days later is a waste of time.

Hélène is introduced to Zofia Tchaïkowska, the orchestra's conductor. The woman who came to pick her up at the Block hands her a violin. Now she has to choose what she's going to play next, because without knowing it, she's about to have an audition.

Fifty-four years later, Hélène still can't explain with certainty what motivated her in such circumstances to play a piece of music as extreme as the *Chaconne*. When she talks about what happened, she says 'and me, like a numbskull, like the idiot that I was, started playing it...', not realizing what kind of character that reveals to us. Was she aware of the stakes – her life – when she decided to give it a try? The *Chaconne* is never a given, she only knows she thought she'd never play again, only to be handed a violin moments later.

A gifted violinist and already a fairly good technician, she could've asked for any score without any real concern, deciphered it on sight, and played it immediately. Yet her choice was to play the *Chaconne*. A terribly difficult piece, which soloists on the violin, as on the guitar, dread because it puts them to the test for different reasons: physically, because it lasts almost twenty minutes; technically, because there are passages of diabolical complexity, requiring total mastery of the instrument and great virtuosity; and finally musically, because without expressiveness and sensitivity, the piece is meaningless.

It's therefore on planet Auschwitz, in the chaos and the unimaginable, that she'll interpret – for what she thinks will be the last time in her life – the quintessence of harmony and balance that comes from Bach's music.

Hélène had arrived in this place only a few hours earlier. On the ramp, her little brother had been led to what she soon learned was the gas chamber. She's dressed in rags, helpless, shaved, and branded like a piece of cattle. She expects to die in a short time. A hundred yards behind her, the crematoriums are smoking, with flames coming out of the fireplace. The Nazis are burning her people. This is the end, and she has to make music as if she's dancing on the corpses. Perhaps for a challenge, in an homage to life, and precisely because it's in a place where only death has its place, she'll play what she loves now more than anything.

She stands in the music room of the orchestra Block. The desks are in a semicircle around the podium where Tchaïkowska usually sits when she thinks she's conducting the ensemble. The bare wooden walls of the Block form a depressing backdrop, and undoubtedly offer very poor acoustics. She tunes the violin she's been given, does a few warm up exercises, then goes for it. She's in her *Chaconne*. Nothing can hurt her anymore, because she's speaking about her inner world, and that's where she finds refuge.

All around, the musicians listen to her more and more intensely as the piece progresses: time in Auschwitz has temporarily stopped and, thanks to her, here they are again, momentarily, back in "civilization". After a while, perhaps on the arpeggio passage, and maybe because it's so beautiful it hurts, Hélène realizes that she's crying. But she continues on because, during the time she's playing, the music even makes it possible to forget Auschwitz, and the misery, and her martyred little brother, and the barking of the SS, the howls of terror, the beatings, and the murders. For all the women present, the music evokes a lost world, a life elsewhere, a family now scattered or destroyed. It crystallizes a peace and an order where the Nazis aren't present, and gives them hope for a brief moment in time. Soon, all the women present weep as she does. Frau Kroner, the 40-year-old "doyenne", weeps with her gentle blue eyes, her face like a fine porcelain doll. Tchaïkowska is crying, and so is her new friend, the woman who got her out of Block 9, Elsa.

On the final chord, silence falls. Hélène has passed her audition. After her period of statutory quarantine has finished, she'll be a "member", just like in any orchestra in the "real world". And fifty years later, on the beach at Knokke, in her beautiful voice and with her articulation so precise, she'll say a little thoughtfully, and a little confused, too, 'You know, come to think of it, I didn't play it very well, that *Chaconne*.'

While her quarantine period continues, Hélène goes to the orchestra's Block in Camp B every morning, before returning later to Block 9 in Camp A, where she must, according to the regulations, be present at the evening rollcall. This means she crosses a large part of Camp B and can see when the rollcall means the preparation of the corpses lined up in front of the barracks on either side of *Lagerstrasse*. Still in rags, and still barefoot, she returns to her Block with the daily reminder of a reality that music can't disguise. Crossing the camp becomes more and more difficult for her as her feet swell, turn blue and become painful. As infection looms, the camp interpreter, Mala Zinetbaum, gives her some comfortable shoes.

Fanny, whom Hélène had known in Mechelen, is still in the quarantine Block. Her mother is with her, but her younger sister and grandmother were gassed on arrival. Attentive to everything happening around her, and still intelligent and energetic, despite the disaster that's befallen her, Fanny's mother sees and understands what's happening to Hélène. She comes to see her one day when she arrives back from a rehearsal: 'could you do something for my daughter? She's a musician like you, she plays the mandolin.'

Hélène is only too happy to be able to try to do for someone else what Elsa has done for her. She asks Tchaïkowska if Fanny can join the orchestra, which, after an audition, is exactly what happens.

These three young girls will cement their friendship with the recognition that they owe their lives to each other. In return, when Fanny's mother dies of typhus sometime after her daughter joins the orchestra, it's Elsa and Hélène who are instructed to tell Fanny that her mother hasn't survived.

This is how the "Belgian Trio" is formed. It will never break, despite the passing of Elsa in 1964, and that of Fanny in 1992. As the last of the three, Hélène still remembers the group, present and alive as ever.

Chapter 4

The Weight of Words

Paris, 10 December 1995

A twisting ache in the back, a vice-like pain in the sternum region, a numb left arm… In my life there's now a *before* and an *after*: before and after the fraction of a second when I thought I was dying, on an operating table at the Lariboisière Hospital, where I said to myself 'ah well!', before shouting and bringing myself back to life. Even there, in the depths of despair, I didn't call for you.

I can't sleep. I'm in my hospital bed in the cardiology department, and the person I'm sharing a room with snores, squeaks, and makes hissing noises while they sleep: noises I didn't even know could be produced by a human chest. One idea keeps me awake all night: the majority of you ended up in Birkenau at that pivotal age towards the end of adolescence, between 16 and 20. I thought about how that moment of becoming an adult was stolen from you by the Nazis and put on hold. I'm older now than you'll ever be, and will forever have an eternally young mother, as if you'd been thrown out of time.

For several months I've been in contact with a documentary maker interested in this story, yours, mine, the orchestra's. Together, we went to meet Violette in Paris, and Hélène in Knokke, and we spoke to her again about the episode surrounding the *Chaconne*. Since then there's been an urge to make a film, or to write a book, or both, with the plot corresponding as much as possible to what these women have been able to tell us, and to what those we don't yet know will say.

Violette and Hélène have already told me about the harm they suffered thanks to the work of one of the other orchestra survivors, Fania Fénelon, whose book *Sursis pour l'orchestre* (Playing for Time) was published in 1976. The book, which was translated into several languages and formed the basis of the screenplay for a TV film written by Arthur Miller, was the subject of controversy at a time when the Shoah was beginning to leave the framework of historical films to be replaced by more "respectable" novels or TV series: *Sophie's Choice, Escape from Sobibor, Holocaust*, etc.

I'd already leafed through Fania's book at the home of one of your brothers. Every page where your name appeared was turned down. The epilogue traced the fate of the orchestra's survivors following the liberation in 1945. When it came to you, I was flabbergasted to read that you'd left for America almost immediately afterwards, got married, and died there a little later. On such a subject as this, if Fania hadn't even bothered to check what she was writing, then surely the book couldn't be taken seriously.

*   *   *

I start working with Violette. She's already indicated to me that she has no hesitation talking to me about it, which I interpret with my usual confidence as meaning she thinks me worthy of listening to her. When we talk, her memory, humour and the richness of her expressions dazzle me. Although she's a little worried from time to time about what I am doing, my approach seems honourable to her, and her support is invaluable to me.

Beyond the serious and sometimes dramatic remarks, however, we don't visit a necropolis. It isn't the atmosphere of a wake. We also laugh a lot, smoke more than we should, drink coffee by the gallons, and eat the cakes that are a little too rich which she made for when I came. Her house often smells of baked apple, cinnamon, eastern-European pastry: real life.

The lively gaze, the defiant look she has when she tells me about the funny or grotesque moments she survived through, they teach me as much about your daily life as the tear-jerking, and not always accurate, documentaries on the same subject.

Birkenau, June 1944

Summer is fast approaching: a Polish summer where it's so hot you suffocate, where the sky is leaden as the land around the camp stagnates into clouds of yellow dust above the Blocks, where the only shade to be offered is under the birches, over there at the back, where the *Sonderkommandos* are struggling to burn gassed corpses in the open air because there are too many for the crematoria to absorb. Wretched tufts of grass persist in growing in the ditches along the *Lagerstrasse*, as time goes by, always in the same routine of the daily massacre.

The transports of Hungarian Jews become less important following the large mass killings that began in April, yet they continue to arrive. Éva Steiner, Lili Mathé and Ibi come from one of these convoys, and they tell us about the Nazi invasion of their country in March, the anti-Jewish measures, and the first deportations. Over at the crematorium, the flames and smoke are less dense now, but the smell remains, however, because there is so little wind. The stench sticks to the women's skin so much that they think they'll never be able to forget it if, by some miracle, they manage to survive at all.

The thirst has become more torturous, too. The working days are longer because it's daylight for longer, and there's no reason for the Nazis to spare the inmates: as long as there's daylight to watch them, they can work. Up at 6 o'clock, with the sun, the inmates return to the camp at 8 o'clock in the evening and go to bed at 10.

One day Maria Mandl, the *Oberaufseherin*, walks into the orchestra's Block, a small smile on her face, and calls to them all. A tall, strong woman, with clear eyes, she represents the "Aryan" ideal that the Nazis wish to promote. It's a striking contrast between this motley group, this Court of Miracles in striped uniforms made up of girls from all over Europe, and this statue in an SS uniform, responsible for the organisation and distribution of death in the women's camp.

She is all of these things and, at the same time, along with Irma Grese, the one who shows them the most interest. She loves music and seems deeply moved when Alma performs. But when she leaves the orchestra's Block she simply returns to the massacre, and that's what none of the girls can understand.

What is this concern for musicians, these second-hand artists? Is it a tolerant benevolence towards what we have created – after all, it is she and Hössler who brought the orchestra together and so it is partly their work – or the distant kindness of a master for its pet? Who knows?

Always accompanied by her two wolfhounds, Grese often stands in front of Yvette when she plays the accordion and mimics it with an almost-human smile. Blonde and pretty, Grese almost seems to want some form of personal connection with her, although this didn't prevent her once, when the mood seizes her, from unleashing her dogs at an inmate and only recalling them once the woman has been torn to shreds.

In a burst of generosity, Mandl has several times distributed packages to those girls in the orchestra who received nothing from the outside, and who are unable to "organize" food supplements, or small amenities such as soap or toothpaste, which are very popular on the camp's black market. One time she even compiles and distributes the parcels personally to the astonished girls.

On this occasion there was another surprise, and a big one at that. 'Some of you have been here for over a year and have never had a chance to leave the camp. I'm sending you out for a walk.'

At first taken aback, the women are soon gripped by anguish, just as they are each time the daily routine is disturbed: now that

Alma is no longer there to protect them, has the order come to liquidate them? Has a more sophisticated way been found to kill them rather than the gas chambers? But then they realize that the Polish women are with them, so it can't be about a "selection", for gas or anything else.

*   *   *

They gather in silence, in their usual columns of five. In front of the gate, two SS guards are waiting for them. The gate opens and they walk out, still a little suspicious, escorted by the two Nazis. There's no truck or machine gun outside, and so they turn right, then right again towards the nearby forest, the birch forest that gave the camp its name. At first silenced by the incredible moment, they soon become emboldened and break ranks. Soon they begin to laugh at the situation, quickly finding themselves in groups that slowly disperse along the road, under the amused gaze of the soldiers, who seem less wild than usual. On the way they meet *Kommandos*, either leaving or returning to the camp, who look at them, astonished. 'It's those skivers from the orchestra again!'

Continuing on their way, they arrive at the forest, behind the camp. A pond seems to invite them to take a swim, and even appears to have been designed just for them. With their final fears having dissipated, and incited by the youngest, they undress and dive into the water. They wade and splash each other, laughing because it's good to be still alive. They surprise themselves in these moments, realizing there might be a little more hope than usual in the possibility of a future, whatever that may be, but without Nazis, without barbed wire, without death. Some even think that for a short time they've shed the stench and misery that always accompanies them.

At the water's edge, slightly embarrassed by all these women in short outfits, the SS keep their distance. It's odd when considering the number of un-dressings they've witnessed, especially when the new inmates arrive. Is one of them even blushing?

After quenching their thirst and bathing their entire bodies, the women dry off on the grass and see something that suddenly puts everything into context: a watchtower, where two guards watch like hawks, before waving invitingly to join them at the top of the tower. Bronia and Szura, the two Ukrainians, climb the ladder, neither intimidated nor worried, while the others continue to chat and frolic in the grass. They rediscover sensations they thought they'd forgotten: the smell of wet earth, the tickle of a blade of grass on the neck, the tingling of an insect that isn't a louse but merely a simple ladybird, and even, perhaps, birdsong.

They discuss Mandl's sudden concern for them. Does she feel the wind is turning? Perhaps this means changes in the camp's regime, the end of the massacres? Rumours have always been rife, some propagated by the Nazis, others from who knows where: the Russians are 100 kilometres away, Hitler is overthrown every week… All the speculations sustain a phantom of a hope, otherwise all that remains is to throw yourself on the electrified barbed wire and put an end to this permanent waking nightmare once and for all.

Then comes the signal for the descent back towards planet Auschwitz, the return to this place which claims them as its own. Bronia and Szura come down from the watchtower, singing at the top of their lungs and staggering a little. They seem to be drunk, the guards having probably given them some vodka. A combination of the heat and a lack of food and alcohol means they can barely stand up.

The others are furious and start to panic. How can they avoid being punished now thanks to these two idiots who can't take their alcohol? Without being too gentle, they grab them by the arms and, half walking, half dragging, return to camp in a tight formation to hide the state of the Ukrainian women. Whether through indulgence, a lack of interest or simple inattention, they pass through the gates of Camp A and Camp B without encountering the slightest problem with the guards. Another walk will be organized by Mandl shortly after, but this one won't give rise to any incidents.

Paris, winter 1996

Throughout the almost fifteen hours of my interviews with Violette, this comes up as a leitmotif: she believes that aside from finding compelling facts about the history of the orchestra, my work is actually articulated and underpinned by a search for you, a search about you. However, I don't want your aura, your shadow, to appear too much in the foreground, because I'm afraid that it'll hide the rest of the story, like the tree hiding the rest of the forest.

Violette isn't fooled. She feels that I've put her, as well as her comrades, those that I know as well as the ones I don't yet know, in a specific place that's not always comfortable to accept, the one where I identify you a little in each of them. Her vitality amazes me, especially how she survived it all. I find in her a joy of living that I didn't manage to feel in you during your lifetime. I have to admit that I admire her, and that admiration seems to weigh on her a bit. She often tells me that the halo I put around her head gives her migraines. I think I can understand where she's coming from. She often feels like I can't see (and how could I?) that aspect of a lottery, of chance, to which she owes her survival. In other words, for her, there's nothing wonderful about the fact that she survived.

To make it easier for me to understand, she tries to illustrate her point by telling me a story. Long before the war, her parents had decided that she had to learn to play an instrument. As her mother used to say, it was something she'd always find useful. Violette wasn't just talking about a Jewish mother, who by definition are usually far-sighted and omniscient, but someone who'd already experienced a major crisis, when Europe was plunged into the doldrums in the early 1930s. As far as she was concerned, having a daughter who played an instrument meant she would eventually be able to make a living playing in cafes or nightclubs, if the need arose. It was simply an additional string to her bow.

Violette told me that fate intervened when choosing her instrument: 'If the piano had been chosen for me, for example, I'm sure I wouldn't be here today, because when I came to join the orchestra, the only piano in the Block had been removed and was probably put in the SS officers' mess.' Fate.

Similarly, when she mentions her complete assimilation by Alma Rosé, the idea of a lottery appears again, this time measured against an event that could've killed her, but which ultimately saved her life: the theft of her shoes in the quarantine Block.

Birkenau, spring/summer 1944
Ever since the arrival of the Hungarian convoys after May 1944, the tempo of the camp has changed and is even accelerating. One, two, or even sometimes three trains arrive every day to unload their share of human misery onto the ramp. The Nazis are overwhelmed, but they must still ensure the massacre continues: after all, their leader has told them that the future of the Reich is at stake.

This is how several thousand, then tens of thousands, of people are murdered every day. The additional crematoriums that have been built still aren't enough to absorb the thousands of bodies that emerge from the gas chambers. The experience and technology amassed by a year and a half of industrial massacre, the precision of the specifications imposed by the authorities, and the technical wizardry of the engineers from *Topf und Söhne*,[8] simply aren't enough. Thanks to the effect of the heat given off from the crematoria, the refractory bricks on the chimneys crack and the

---

8. A German engineering company founded in 1878. As well as making weapons shells and military vehicles during the Second World War, it was one of the twelve companies that designed and built crematoria ovens for concentration camps during the Holocaust, including the ventilation systems for the gas chambers at Birkenau.

scrap metal supporting them twists, meaning the ovens can no longer operate at full efficiency. Once again, what raw materials can't withstand, men will have to endure: the *Sonderkommandos* burn the overflow from the crematoria out in the open, then spread the ashes in a pond dug for this specific purpose.

All the "ancillary services" that the Nazis have grafted onto the gas chambers, *Kanada* in particular, are crumbling under the surplus. The maniacal surveillance by the *Kapos* isn't enough to prevent items from starting to circulate in the camp among the men and women, including diamonds, gold, dollars, Swiss francs etc. All these little treasures that were hidden away by those who are now dead, when they still believed that they were going to work "elsewhere"; goods hidden in luggage, in the linings of clothes, on the bodies of the tortured.

For a while, the camp's shadow economy is shattered, but not for too long. The basic exchange currency remains the same: it's always the bread ration. Staggering exchanges are taking place: a half-starved inmate, who had been a banker in another life, "discovers" a small bag containing diamonds that's been miraculously saved from the multiple searches and checks carried out on the trapped men and women in Birkenau. He exchanges it for a raw potato with a kitchen worker, loosely removes the earth stuck to the skin and immediately gobbles it up. The two men seem satisfied with their transaction: the world is turning completely upside down.

The clothes and furs brought by the Hungarians are sorted, like the rest, so that the best, the most beautiful, are sent to Germany, although only when they're not diverted by the SS guards for their own use.

For the girls in the orchestra, this massive influx of Nazi-stolen goods has unexpected side effects, as they manage to obtain small gifts such as pocket mirrors, combs and hairbrushes through their comrades in *Kanada*. Violette obtains a small bottle of lavender water which she carefully places in the music cabinet, but is unable to find it again soon after.

Mandl, always so unpredictable in her madness, gives them nightgowns, silks, satin, lace; an incredible luxury of lingerie that they wear with more pleasure than ever, having never worn such clothes before, even when they were free. They compare items, showing each other the embroidery, the fastenings, the moiré of this satin, the lightness of that silk.

This strange and bizarre situation gives them the giggles. They laugh even more as they imagine what the reactions and first words of a parachutist – hopefully American – will be as he crosses over the roof of their Block and encounters the improbable bunch of kids that they are. Bunk beds? Silk nightgowns? This can't be an extermination camp. Surely it's a boarding school for young girls. And, given the richness of the linen, a boarding school for young girls in Switzerland at that. Their daily life is strewn with this cocktail of horror and laughter.

Violette still remembers a joke she made up. One morning, she goes to see her friends and asks them coldly: 'Do you know what two SS guards say to each other in the morning when they wake up?' Most of them are wide-eyed, except for one or two who have already guessed and start to laugh like crazy.

'So… is that gauze?'[9]

Having guessed the answer before she told me the punchline, my laughter was a bit constrained. However, Violette looked satisfied – even in places like Birkenau you could thumb your nose at death and the Nazis – and the pride she had in claiming this as having been made up on the spot, as well as the offended look of some that she mimed to me at the same time, were certainly worth a medal.

* * *

---

9. Translator's note: In French, gas (*gaz*) and gause (*gaze*) are pronounced very similarly.

They make fun of themselves and their torturers. 'We must be privileged, every time they gas us they put a double dose in so that we go up faster!' One inmate says. Mockingly, Lotte compares the colour of the flames produced by their respective corpses in the crematorium with Sylvia, who sleeps above her. 'I'm tall and fat so the flame I'll make will be a greasy yellow. You're a little microbe and so thin you'll just make a bluish gassy flame!'

Caught up in the whirlwind, they brazenly fight in their own way against despair and depression through derision and the absurd, and through music. The French women like to improvise singing several songs by Charles Trenet or Jean Sablon, including *J'attendrai*, which had been a big hit in 1940-41, when they'd pined for the prisoners of war who never returned from the Stalags.

Little Hélène, a DIY genius, gets her hands on a whole stock of orange tissue paper. Part of it is, of course, used for toilet paper, but she dyes the remaining paper blue and manages to create berets like those worn by the *Kriegsmarine* sailors, and the girls sing a vaguely saucy song, *Unter die rote Laterne von Sankt Pauli* (Under the Red Lantern of Saint Pauli). The Nazi's navy is being crushed by the Allies around the globe, so why not represent that symbolically in Birkenau?!

One evening, someone (is it Violette, Little Hélène or someone else, it doesn't matter), has an idea: 'What if we organized a beauty contest?' Excitedly, the Francophones get to work. Categories will include who has the most beautiful mouth, the most beautiful eyes, the most beautiful legs, the most beautiful breasts, the most beautiful face, with votes being decided by a round of applause. The Germans and Poles, being either more reserved or more shocked, don't participate, while the Ukrainians, as usual, smile and don't understand what's going on. The jury is established, and a whole evening passes by. One more evening that the Nazis can't take away from them.

Fifty years later, no one remembers the winners. After I insisted heavily, Yvette, slightly confused, confesses and laughs a little saying that she won a prize: 'But they were all so nice to me! They made sure my hair wasn't cut too short...'

Paris, autumn 1996
Building on her previous comments, Violette tells me about some grotesque episodes from their life in the camp: moments of bewilderment at the incomprehensible, but funny and heroic ones, too. There's no armed resistance or self-sacrifice, and God knows the courage it took for the women who worked in the arms factory to smuggle explosives sewn into their hems into the camp. Four of these women were hanged for this in front of the entire camp. Then there were the members of *Sonderkommando No. 3*, who blow up the crematorium and the gas chamber to which they were assigned.

Violette tells me stories of small acts of heroism that occurred on a daily basis, of times when the sub-humans who were to be massacred regained, if only for a moment, their status as men and women, by making fun of their torturers. These stories provide images of life, not just those of simple biological survival...

Birkenau, 30 October 1944
They're all gathered together in the Block: Jews on the right, non-Jews on the left. It looks glaringly like the selections on the ramp. For Anita, this can only mean one thing: they're going to be gassed. The simplicity and suddenness of what takes place is striking. Anita only thinks of one thing: she won't have time to warn Renate.

After Alma's death in April, they all know, more or less, that something has changed. The orchestra continues to perform military marches at the gate, but there are fewer and fewer "sauna" concerts, if any at all. The music is still the same and they still know their parts inside and out – Alma fought hard enough for that – and the violin solos are now played by the wonderful Hélène. However, there's no longer that constant search for perfection that was Alma's trademark, and which gave the orchestra its soul. Now that Alma's gone, everyone plays rather mechanically.

To top it off, Kramer has appointed Sonia Vinogradova to replace Alma as the conductor, which is a mistake. No matter how good a pianist she is, she lacks Alma's talent and charisma, and flutters on her podium instead of conducting. Of course, Fania should've been appointed because she has the skill to do it and while she continues to work on new pieces with the orchestra in order to renew the repertoire, it's still Sonia who takes on the responsibility of conductor. No doubt the Nazis have decided that from now on the orchestra should be led by a non-Jew, and now the standard of the group has been declining for some time.

A few weeks earlier, Kramer ordered that rehearsals will only take place in the morning, and in the afternoon they are given "productive" work involving knitting and hemming pieces of fabric in their Block for who knows what purpose. The work still provides a place of escape, but it also marks a turning point in the life of the orchestra, which is no longer a *Kommando* like any other. Indeed, the Nazis have probably just assessed the functional and bureaucratic elements of the situation: after all, only a few instruments are needed to count women and make them march in time; a bass drum, cymbals and a few fifes can largely do the trick. There's no longer any need to keep forty-five women warm and secure. As for the SS officers' recreational afternoons, they'll just have to find gramophones.

*   *   *

Then arrives confirmation of a persistent rumour that's been circulating throughout the camp for several weeks, as they learn with anguish of their transfer "elsewhere". Without exception, they must now return all the "treasures" they've collected since their entry into the orchestra, including their comfortable clothes and shoes. The blankets and sheets, meanwhile, will remain on the beds in the Block. The individual boxes where they put their cutlery and the few accessories whose possession, nevertheless, marks their difference in status and separates them from the world of the other prisoners. Their combs, toothbrushes and soaps will all remain in their places in the cabinet.

Hilde miraculously manages to hold on to a few objects, including a French diary from 1939 covered in black velvet, along with a small golden fountain pen. The diary belonged to Alma and there are a few hand-written notes inside, as well as an address. On the notes page, Hilde writes out a poem by Rainer Maria Rilke, *Der Ritter* (The Knight).

Anita, whether more practical or luckier, manages to hold on to a red angora wool sweater, "obtained" from *Kanada* for a fortune in bread rations. In exchange for the clothes stored in the depot, they are given items that have been worn and brought back by several inmates before them, now long dead and forgotten. Touching those coarse disinfected clothes reassures them a little, but not too much.

Once dressed, they're directed towards the gate, then towards the guard post on the left, then left again, towards the ramp and the gas chambers. However, they're relieved when told to stop at the ramp, and barked at to wait there. Renate, seeing her sister leave, joins the group without further ado. Soon a long procession of inmates joins them on the ramp, along with a train. It's good to be transferred to another camp.

They stand a little apart from the mass of prisoners and climb into one of the cattle wagons at the end of the convoy. Kramer has assigned them a special wagon just for them; even while being transferred, they still have privileges and won't travel like the others, packed to the point of suffocation. Once in their wagon, they finally realize that they're leaving Birkenau, but not, as the saying goes, by the chimney, like so many of their companions before them. The enormity of the situation makes them silent and pensive for a moment.

The trip lasts several days, during which time they sleep, bicker and chat like schoolgirls going on holiday. The weather has already turned very cold and they try to keep warm as best they can, blowing air onto each other's backs. They all wonder where they're going to end up and what'll happen to them. A rumour had been going around the camp and there had been talk of a former military camp, somewhere called Bergen-Belsen…

The women know the Russians are approaching from the east, and that the Anglo-Americans have been in Europe since June, so they estimate: 'At best the war will be over by the beginning of 1945, so what can the SS do with us now, other than slaughter us?'

For some time now, the journeys described by the transports of deportees have made them dizzy. Whole families of detainees have arrived in Birkenau from Terezín (Theresienstadt) in Czechoslovakia, and several of them were musicians. Most were gassed pretty quickly, often as soon as they arrived on the ramp. And while other transports continue to arrive from all over Europe, at the same time prisoners are being sent west. It all smacks of a debacle and feverish improvisation: something the Nazis are clearly not experts in. Like all deportees in their situation, the women are aware that they're in a race against time, and that they have little chance of surviving. However, before long they find themselves hoping: 'But, what if…'

In the wagon they usually sing, often for hours, to try to boost their morale. And as they no longer have their instruments, they sing the parts they would normally play. Yvette's clear voice imitates a double bass, while Violette's is a little lighter – she is trying to imitate Zara Leander – to mimic the pizzicatti violin, and Lily's shrill voice simulating the accordion is hilarious.

Their guards aren't SS or *feldgendarmerie* [military police], but "normal" soldiers, mainly old men from the *Volksturm*. Germany has started to scrape the barrel and recall reservists or men who'd been demobilized, as well as mobilizing the children of the Hitler Youth. The guards don't systematically bark out orders, but talk to them like men talk to most human beings, and are obviously touched by the women's youth and bravery. In reality, this is more to do with the acceptance of their inevitable death, but the guards, the "real people", don't know this and, in a sublime piece of irony, they'll empty the toilet bucket that's been assigned to their wagon throughout the journey. For a short time, at least, the world – the Nazi's world – is turned upside down.

At the end of their journey they arrive in the middle of the forest. They form a column of five and advance through the trees towards an unknown destination. Anita and Big Hélène are in the front row of the procession, which eventually comes to a clearing. In the distance, gunshots echo endlessly and Anita notices an arrow signpost, written in Gothic letters. A tear runs down her cheek. Hélène, who's never seen her cry before, is stunned, and looks at her questioningly. Anita shows her the sign, which reads "Juden Schiesstand" (Jewish Shooting Range). Exhausted, and with a bad feeling in the pit of their stomachs, they walk on. They're not going to give in like this. Expecting to fall into a mass grave which will serve as their burial place, they continue on their way and arrive at an immense, open piece of ground, surrounded by the eternal electrified barbed wire fence and watchtowers.

The sign hadn't read "Juden Schiesstand", but "Zu dem Schiesstand" (To the Shooting Range), and Violette, who'd been just as confused as the others, feels the same relief as her comrades. They'd been toys in the Nazi's killing machine for so long that it was only afterwards they realized this would've been absurd, even for the Nazis. Why make them travel for several days by train and then shoot them, when the gas chamber was only 100 metres away from their Block in Birkenau?!

They stopped on a military training ground and were separated into groups; happy not to be directly sent to the shooting range, but desperate that the same nightmare was repeating itself. Will it never end? Seeing where they are, and anxious not to witness the deaths of all her companions, Anita sighs: 'I hope I'm not the last to die here...'

After leaving the insane and organized hell of Birkenau, they've arrived in the chaotic hell of Belsen.

Bergen-Belsen, 4 November 1944

Violet clenches her teeth. She's just realized that it's her parents' wedding anniversary, and that exactly one year ago, she was leaving the *Revier* after contracting typhus. For almost a year and a half she's been pushed here and there like rubbish under a rake, at the discretion of the executioners. It's pretty much clear to everyone now that Germany is losing the war and that the Nazis are going to die; them and their filthy Third Reich. On the train from Birkenau they'd been able to see the bombed and smoking German cities through the slats of the wagon. 'Now it's their turn!' However busy they may be with their own lives, they still saw "real people", not skeletons dressed in the deportee's *pasiak* (striped uniform). In addition to their misery, the vision of a universe without the SS and their dogs grips their hearts with envy and nostalgia.

Violette, who often discussed with Hélène as to what "freedom" meant to her, had found it in the symbolic form of a green apple, juicy and a little sour. For her part, Hélène was thinking of scrambled eggs with a fresh *pistolet*, a Belgian bun that she'd not seen, let alone tasted, for years. Somewhere on a station platform, perhaps in Katowice, Violette saw someone carrying a shopping bag with apples in it!

She seemed to have caught every illness possible in Birkenau: furunculosis, typhus, scabies, dysentery... But life – and luck –

hadn't let her down. And not only did she still have luck, she still had energy, too. The sight of a defeated Germany would even cheer her up a bit – 'This is the home stretch, those bastards are going to die, as well!' – if only it weren't for the uncertainty about their immediate future.

*   *   *

When they arrive in Belsen, they notice something important. The portion of the camp allocated to them is almost entirely bare, with only a few water pipes here and there. No Blocks have been built, just a few barracks set up by ragged Soviet prisoners. They find themselves in a type of landscape that's more familiar to them, more temperate. They are surrounded by trees and the ground is no longer the yellowish mud of Birkenau, but a good black earth, with grass and insects. And is that birdsong they can hear? But above all, there are no smoking chimneys, these concrete buildings of which all knew their purpose. There are no gas chambers here! A possible ray of hope in the darkness.

When they pass through the gate of the camp, they quickly become disillusioned. Renate, Anita's sister, notices a man with a *Kapo*'s armband scratching the bottom of a container for food. 'If they're reduced to that, we're not going to eat every day,' she grumbles.

For the first few nights they sleep in a military tent, or rather under a tarpaulin, with several hundred of them piled in together on the damp ground. The Nazis, these so-called masters of organisation, have no plans for housing the mass of inmates arriving from Birkenau. In vain, Hilde and Anita try to make sure that people don't trample on them.

A large storm breaks out and, one night, the wind flattens the tarpaulin. Cold and soaked to the bone, they spend the rest of the night out in the rain, huddled together like a herd of sheep in a storm. For Anita, to have survived that night without catching a cold, when any normal person would've developed pneumonia and some other curse, was both a mystery and a miracle. It might not be Birkenau, but the SS are still there. And if it isn't hell, it's at least purgatory.

The day after the storm, they wade through a sea of mud. The thin military blankets that were given to them when they left Birkenau aren't enough to keep them warm, and neither does the very meagre broth (in reality little more than hot water), which is given to them as coffee.

After the months of protection conferred by their membership of the orchestra, they've now suddenly fallen back in with the rest and, like the others, are nothing more than deportees. After a few days they're taken to safety in the shoe warehouse, then finally to a barracks previously occupied by Soviet prisoners. Anita wonders if the Nazis killed them in order to make room for the women?

Bergen–Belsen, winter 1944–45

They strive to stay together, at least in their Blocks, as the chances of being assigned to different work *Kommandos* mean they're scattered throughout the camp. One of the bizarre tasks they're assigned involves weaving strips of greenish cellophane paper, but no one is quite sure as to what it'll be used for. However, it turns out that it eventually forms part of the camouflage netting used by the *Wehrmacht*.

As she speaks French, German and Hungarian, Violette will soon be entrusted with a group of 200 women, mostly Hungarians. Now that she's a *Kapo*, she takes Fania as her "assistant" in order to protect her a little, as well as meaning they can help support each other.

To pass the time, Fania has some success with a deck of pocket cards she's somehow managed to get hold of. One day, upon seeing her approach, an *Aufseherin* makes contact with her in the usual way – a slap in the face – then asks her what she's doing.

'I'm telling fortunes.'

'You know how to do that? Do it for me!' the Nazi orders.

Fania assumes the searching and solemn look required in such circumstances. She cuts the deck, takes out the cards, examines them for a long time, then begins to look bored: 'You have family somewhere, don't you?'

The other woman nods, tense. Fania escalates the anxiety by hesitating before she next speaks. 'The cards, I'm not sure, I could be wrong, you shouldn't always believe them…' The increasingly worried *Aufseherin* urges Fania to tell her about her future, and so she begins to make doomsday predictions about the SS. The *Aufseherin*'s husband will no doubt die on the Eastern Front, her family will be flattened by the bombs and die in excruciating pain, her dog will catch the plague, she herself will be shot, etc. etc.

Violet watches the scene, concerned. This Nazi isn't stupid enough to swallow all of that. She'll react. She'll hit Fania, or even shoot her. She's afraid for her friend, but at the same time finds it difficult to keep a straight face. She'll have to wait until the *Aufseherin* has left the Block, dismayed, before she can laugh out loud with Fania, who's naturally quite proud of her efforts. Another small act of daily courage.

*   *   *

Life, or whatever has taken its place, is fairly regulated. At the end of December, Kramer takes over as director of Belsen. It's considered a promotion, as at Birkenau he still reported administratively to the commander of Auschwitz-I. A few days before the end of the year 1944 – no one remembers precisely when – during one of the daily rollcall sessions, the women receive a shock: Kramer has recognized them. They're still fairly united, having decided to preserve the group they'd formed, *die Kapelle* (the orchestra) as much as possible from among the mass of other inmates. Now, a senior member of the SS has distinguished and recognized a handful of Jews in this crowd of Jews marked only with numbers, with no names or faces.

He walks up to them and immediately asks if they're able to play, without sheet music or a conductor, some of the pieces they used to perform with the Birkenau orchestra. Without hesitation, they all nod. Alma has trained them enough to be able to play in any weather and in any conditions, including when their mind is elsewhere, either thinking about food, or a way to "organize" a ration of extra soup... There's no real risk: it can give them some small material advantages and, above all, a musical morning. Even if it means being with the SS, it's still an opportunity to escape the depressing framework of the *Lager* and its fatal and exhausting routine, if only for a few hours. For months, even years now, they've learned the art of day-to-day survival and how to adapt.

Ever the zealous bureaucrat, Kramer takes note and walks away. They are collected the following Sunday. The violinists, the singers, Anita the cellist, and – memories differ – Lili. Were the flautists present? Nobody knows anymore. They're taken to the officers' mess, outside the camp grounds, where the instruments await them. They must prepare as Alma taught them, and do what they're there to do. And so once again, without the women being able to do anything about it, the scandal of music in the death camps begins again.

After the concert, Kramer asks for volunteers among the musicians to carry the instruments back to his house. A few, including Violette, Anita, Big Hélène and Elsa, step forwards and, duly supervised by the guard dogs, proceed to Kramer's house. They're probably a little curious to see what it is like inside a Nazi home. Flora Schrijvers had formerly served as governess to Kramer's two children at Birkenau and had told them a little about it. This time, when they enter the house, they can see for themselves that it's ordinary, petty-bourgeois and rather harmless. But a surprise is waiting for them: in Kramer's dining room, a large bowl of rice pudding has been prepared. There are spoons stuck in the rice, and Kramer invites them to sit down. As they eat in silence, Kramer does something insane: he turns up his gramophone, puts on a Bach record and quietly walks out of the room. No one will believe them when they tell their story after returning to the Block. Bach and rice pudding? From a Nazi? Get away!

As Anita would say later, in an English film dedicated to her: 'Who can understand these people?'

Chapter 5

The Orchestra

Brussels, winter 1996

I'm terribly afraid of hurting Hélène. She's made it clear to me what the cost of bringing up these memories in front of me does to her. She's also told me that I'm the last person she'll ever talk to about it, but that she'll make the effort for me because I'm my mother's son. She recognizes my need to access a heritage that's been hidden away for far too long. I'll never forget this honour that she's given me, this recognition of my right to know what happened. She's agreed to speak, and yet her vulnerability leads me to take maximum precautions with her.

As she wrote in her article, she worries that she, too, will be struck by some form of cancer. She says it'll be "her turn", because cancer seems to strike an exaggeratedly high number of people returning from deportation: you, Fanny, Little Hélène, Big Julie, and so many others. Does the curse even continue to cross the generational mark in some cases? One of Fanny's daughters died of the disease a few months after her mother, and her remaining daughter now has to struggle with that as well. Will it ever stop?

It's a small world!

While on holiday in Miami for a few days, Hélène and Paul, her husband, have rented an apartment in a "luxury" residence, which includes ultra-sophisticated appliances, modern amenities in the building, and a swimming pool on the ground floor. The weather is nice, but not warm enough for sunbathing in the Florida sunshine.

Instead, they go shopping and play bridge in the afternoon (Paul is a formidable player), while Hélène is just beginning to learn the "stayman'" convention. In the evenings they go out: they both love to dance, and Miami offers a wealth of possibilities in that area. After two weeks they return to Belgium and leave the apartment for Paul's sister. The weather is fine, and, among other activities, she's able to go down to the pool without any problems.

Sat on a deckchair by the water, a tall, flamboyant woman in her forties with a dark complexion and red hair is reading her book. Paul's sister approaches her and sees a tattooed number on her left arm. She notices the number is very close to her own and so dares to speak to her: they are both survivors of Birkenau and find they can exchange their common experience through a common language, French. Although Greek, the other woman has a good accent and rolls her "Rs" in a way that sounds pleasant to the ear. After a while Paul's sister talks about Hélène, her sister-in-law. The other woman immediately comes to life and becomes more talkative. She knew her very well, they were together in the orchestra, and tells Paul's sister to say that Big Julie sends her regards and will contact her as soon as possible!

Sadly, Hélène will take a little while to get back in touch, and Big Julie will later die of cancer.

* * *

It's often the same topic of conversation with Violette and Hélène. They continue, in many respects, to live as those condemned to death, on borrowed time, despite the defeat of the Third Reich and its allies, Pétainists, Rexists and various fascists, and despite the scattering to the four winds of the executioners who tortured and traded them so skilfully. Such a position leads them, in a rather contradictory way, to combine a great joy of living, of making the most of any big or small misfortunes that might strike them from day to day – something that life certainly hasn't been stingy in throwing at them – to a certain kind of fatalism. As Violette often says: '*que sera sera*'... It's a burden that everyone must handle in their own way. Violette gives me the impression that she manages it through distancing and humour, which is often black. Hélène still seems to be suffering from sleepless nights. There isn't a day goes by, she tells me, when she doesn't think about *that*. I sense a certain fragility, which makes me want to protect her, the survivor, from the effects of conjuring these memories.

What strikes me most about Hélène are her voice and eyes. Those blue eyes, clear and perpetually astonished: the eyes of a teenage girl who experienced all that while still retaining some kind of fantasy. That 16-year-old who, 'like an idiot', was only thinking of one thing, her violin, in the quarantine Block, is still there standing in front of me. Her voice is also quite extraordinary. I listen to it in an interview for an entire afternoon, and wonder where I'd heard a sound like that before, so warm, and superbly articulated. In the evening, when listening to my cassettes again, it comes back to me: a viola da gamba, the musical instrument that, after the guitar, has the most effect on me. It's less precise than the violin, with deep, persistent yet sure notes, whose sounds never fail to move me.

There's an object in her living room that attracts me, the origin and meaning of which I've never dared to ask. The back of a violin, complete with holes and a little burned, is encased in transparent resin. I see it as a symbol, a reminder of a shattered passion, of an existence devoted to music, brought to a halt by disaster. When she talks about you, there's a smile, a hint of nostalgia, but also a whine in her voice, which mellows more. For me, Hélène's voice really is like music. She undoubtedly misses you, and will continue to do so until her last day on Earth.

She talks about her career, her life, how she first met you and Fanny, then her meeting with Alma. Her memory isn't as structured and detailed as that of Violette, but it's just as evocative and powerful. In her mind, the feelings of a young girl and her incomprehension in front of the massacre she was witness to, mingle with the absurdity of her position. From being a puppet with a number destined for the slaughterhouse and oven, she went straight to having the status of a privileged member of the Birkenau "aristocracy". I find myself wondering how, when caught up in such madness, she had, and indeed you had, the resources not to give up completely.

Birkenau, spring/summer 1944
It really is an orchestra of odds and ends. The most experienced of them – not to mention the oldest – Frau Kroner, had played the flute in a symphony orchestra, who knows where. Helga Schiessel sang and played the drums in a brewery orchestra in Munich. Lily Assael played the piano in a variety hall orchestra. As for Fania, well, according to some of her accounts she'd toured with the Opéra-Comique de Paris, while other times she agreed that she'd only sung in cabarets all over Europe, but not just anywhere, only the best places. Her artist's name, in the other world, was "Fania la Perla". Small, lively and intelligent, she's a very good musician, and her "handicap" of having too small hands had been the only obstacle preventing her from becoming a concert pianist. She's extremely cultured, with a prodigious memory and a devastating sense of humour.

Apart from Alma, these were the only professional musicians. The rest of the women are therefore predominantly Jewish and speak Polish, Dutch, Czech, French or German. They're an incredible group of musicians, not exactly "expert" on the whole, and have been thrown together by circumstance. Some, such as the Ukrainians, are guitarists, while others such as Violette, Fanny and you, are second-hand violinists or mandolinists.

From all over Europe, they've been poured together down the gigantic bottleneck of Auschwitz, a place that its first commander, Höss, called *anus mundi* [the word's anus], due to the fact that here was where the operation to "disinfect" the world by disposing of its "waste" (Jews, homosexuals, Gypsies), would take place.

Nazi technocrats had made an art of extracting torture from all their businesses: making women walk in step to the sound of military marches to be able to count the living and the dead easier, and keeping daily accounts of the productivity of their extermination work, was not, according to their logic, a bad idea. What's absurd is that in this place, where music had absolutely no right to be – can you imagine Schubert or Dvoràk in Auschwitz? –, this group of forty young women and girls had succeeded in making good music, music that some even say they had fun playing: can you imagine people enjoying themselves at Auschwitz? Yet it was this music that saved their lives: of the forty or so that Alma made into a real orchestra, only six never came back. Compared to the other number of survivors, such a figure is unheard of.

*   *   *

At first I didn't know how or by whom the orchestra was started. By deduction, I thought there must have been a core of rhythmic instruments, percussions and cymbals, a few flutes perhaps, to give a cheerful and military, perhaps even "perky", air to the whole arrangement. With this as the starting nucleus, the violin players, guitars, and voices would undoubtedly then have gathered around. The Nazi's desire to have a real orchestra, rather than a few instrumentalists playing a concert with what approximated music, was proved by the arrival of Alma, and by the facilities given to her by Hössler, then Kramer, the two camp commanders, allowing her to shape the group as she pleased.

For these women from Birkenau, the process which, under normal conditions, takes decades to set up, the constitution of a musical group whose qualities no longer depend on individuals but on the collective whole, had been condensed into just a few months. They now play military marches in the morning and evening in front of the gate, as the *Kommandos* depart and return from their work outside the camp in the surrounding armaments factories, on road construction sites, or railway tracks.

In order to distract the SS, exhausted by their daily work of administering death, the orchestra are a new kind of jukebox. Indeed, it's not uncommon that between massacres, Mengele, Hössler, or Tauber arrive, give Alma a vague nod, and point to the programme prepared for the occasion, either one, two or three pieces of music. Relaxed by their musical sojourn, they then return to their work. A couple of times Mengele will ask for Anita to perform the solo in Schumann's *Traümerei*, expressing regret that Bach isn't in the orchestra's repertoire. Hélène is unable to lift her head to look at this man, so scared is she of what he represents. Violette, on the other hand, doesn't miss a beat. "The Angel of Death" has a little Latin lover side, Charles Boyer style, which clashes somewhat with the overall picture…

By some sadistic or simply administrative aberration, they also have to give concerts to prisoners on Sundays, the one day of the week when they're not working. In good weather, the concerts are held in the barbed wire space between Camp A and Camp B, then in the "sauna" or at the *Revier* when it's too bad or too cold. There are even orchestral exchanges, when the women's orchestra go to give concerts in the men's camp and vice versa.

* * *

Their setup, no doubt developed by Alma to better structure the ensemble, is always the same, whether in the music room at the Block, or outside. Hélène, known as Big Hélène, is first violin, along with Helena Dunicz, one of the orchestra's young non-Jewish Poles. Then, sometime later, they're joined by Ibi, a blonde and pretty Hungarian, who, before the war, studied classical music and already plays very well, and Lili Mathé, who specializes more in gypsy music: a long time later, back in the "real world", she'll have her own gypsy orchestra. Ibi and Lili had arrived during the large convoys of Hungarian Jews in the spring of 1944.

In front of them, on the other side of the semi-circle, with Alma's podium in the centre, is the second violin desk. That's where you, Elsa, sit, and Hélène will always feel indebted to you for having gone to look for her at Block 9, and will consequently love you like a sister. You sit between Little Hélène and Little Fanny, so named to differentiate them from Big Hélène and Fanny, a mandolin player and the third member of the "Belgian Trio", which she forms with you and Hélène. To the left of the first violins are the third violins: Violette, Wisha Zatorska and Pane (Madame) Irena Lagowska, both Polish and non-Jewish. Left again, and slightly behind, sit the group of mandolins: Big Fanny, Rachela Olewski and Julie. Facing the podium, on the left, are the accordionists: Lily, Flora and, for a while, Yvette, Lily's sister. On the right are the flautists: Frau Kroner, Carla, her sister Sylvia, and Ruth. Behind them are the drums, played by Helga, and the double bass. To the right of the podium are the guitars: Bronia, Marila, Szura, and Margott Vetrovcova. Behind Alma are the singers, Éva Steiner, Claire Monis, Lotte Lebedowa, Fania and Éva Stojowska. To the women's delight, Anita will be integrated into the orchestra as a cellist, a few days after her arrival at Auschwitz in November 1943. She has a solid style, having played the instrument for ten years, and will sit front of Alma, slightly to her left.

They don't have to play outside in all weathers. Among other benefits, Alma has been able to keep them from playing when it rains as it's not good for the instruments. Nor should they play music when it's too cold, as the musicians can't afford to catch frostbite.

Before they start to play near the gates of Camp A, they arrive by marching, at a walking pace, in rows of five, carrying their instruments under their arms like tools or weapons. On these occasions, twice a day, they all have to wear the orchestra's own "uniform", rather than that of the other prisoners: the white cotton scarf, white blouse, and the navy blue skirt. When it's cold, they manage to wear something warm under the blouse, a jumper that's been "organized" in *Kanada*, or whatever other item of clothing stops the wind. The surrounding landscape is as flat as a pancake and neither the birches nor the concrete blocks to the north of the camp, where prisoners are murdered and burned all day long, can protect them from the wind.

Once sat in position on their stools in front of their wooden music stands, they play all ten military marches in their repertoire one after another, including Schubert's *Military March* and Berlioz's *Rákóczi March* among others, not to mention, of course, the more "specialized" marching songs of the German Army, such as *Erika*, *Ich Hat'ein Kammerad*, and the song which has ominously resonated across Europe, *Heili Heilo Heila*.

* * *

The inmates of Camp B are already in their column of five, organized by the working *Kommando*, with the *Kapo* in the lead. With the exception of those who leave to work in the region's arms factories, dressed in striped uniforms, the rest simply wear rags that were given to them upon arrival. When they hear the music echoing from 800 metres away, they set off together and march on.

From the SS guard post directly in front of the orchestra, they're counted on departure and arrival, meaning the registers and accounts are thus kept up to date. As each inmate is leased to companies that pay 7 Reichmarks per person per day, the camp administration needs to know exactly how much to charge for this army of slaves if they want to exploit it. In the mornings, the procession shuffles the few hundred metres to the main gate, before resuming a "normal" gait and pace; in the evenings, they have to wait until they get to Camp B before breaking ranks.

The arrangement of the orchestra is always the same: a semi-circle around the podium, where Alma conducts with her back to the SS guard post and the parade of slaves. The music stands for the different instruments are arranged in the same places as they are in the music room. The guitarists and singers, slightly superfluous when performing military music, remain in the Block after having removed the musicians' stands and stools.

They play as best they can, because that's what Alma demands, but at the same time they look at the marching women and exchange signs or winks with those they know as they pass by. It allows them to see how they're doing on a daily basis, and whether they're holding up. As they pass in front of the orchestra, in front of their friends, some feel the need to pull themselves up, even if they're exhausted or sick, and it's often good for morale. But sometimes this musical parade turns into a nightmare, such as when girls are brought back on a stretcher from work, or when one of them is torn to pieces by a dog, the memory which sometimes still prevents Hilde from sleeping.

The privilege of not having to break stones to build roads or railways, or of not being beaten, starving, or exhausted, as well as not being piled on top of each other in Blocks, doesn't always engender kindness from their fellow prisoners. There are some among the inmates who look on them with envy or hatred: they're only human. After all, once the inmates of the *Aussenkommandos* have passed, the musicians will play music in the shelter of their Block, without a *Kapo* to "goad" them with kicks or with the distinctive instrument of their role, the club, the use of which means any order given is immediately understood by the victim, whatever their language.

*   *   *

As first violin, Big Hélène sits on the far end of the semi-circle that the musicians form around Alma. She's the one that the inmates see best because she's closer to the ranks as they march past. Everyone knows her. With her blond curly hair, round face, big eyes, and her youth, they all think she's cute: a bit like a mascot, at least for those who don't consider her to be a collaborator, having obtained her musician's privileges by who knows what means.

One day, she hears someone shouting during the procession: 'It can't be, Hélène, is it you?' She knows that voice, and can put a name to it as soon as she sees who's calling her: it's Ida, one of her childhood friends. Ida's father owned a cinema in Brussels where the girls would spend whole afternoons, so far away and so long ago, in the other world.

As always, when an external event intervenes to remind them that another planet had existed beyond the barbed wire, the kind of existence they all lead here in order to survive, where you must steal one minute and then another from the killing machine, it all shatters immediately and gives way to raw suffering. Brought back to Brussels and her former life by the presence of Ida, Hélène immediately stops playing and bursts into incompressible sobs: the fragile little bubble offered to her by music, even military music, has just exploded.

Hélène has another surprise when they return to the Block. Mad with rage, Alma administers a masterful pair of slaps to her in the form of consolation and shakes her strongly: 'You're not here to cry or dream, but to play! Whatever happens, keep your nerves in check. The show must go on!'

Beyond the radical nature of the lesson, Hélène is forced to admit the relevance of Alma's remark and never blamed her for her reaction: if they start rehashing memories from before, they're lost. There's no more music, no more orchestra, no more protection. Auschwitz wins for good.

Put back on the right track by Alma's slap in the face, Hélène will remain a dreamy, generous and somewhat idealistic child. Meanwhile, she decides to try something for Ida. The day after the incident, the person in charge of the work organisation at Auschwitz, *Arbeitsdienstführer* Tauber, enters the Block. He nods briefly at Alma, asks for the programme, and checks off a few pieces of music: he's looking for something to do. Tauber is a thick brute. Tall, blond, with clear, hard eyes in an angular face, he's killed inmates in demented fits of anger with kicks, punches or clubs. He also invented an original pastime: he holds his whip at a certain height from the ground and makes women jump over it, before using his club to kill those who are too weak to manage to jump "properly".

As in any orchestra, after the musical interlude the instruments are put back in their cases after being cleaned, resin put on the strings, bows loosened etc. As Tauber prepares to leave, Hélène approaches him and dares to speak to him. Shocked, everyone falls silent. 'Prisoner 51848, Officer. I have a request to make.' It's extremely rare for an inmate to speak to a member of the SS. She has to stand to attention, showing the highest respect to the bully, but not look him in the eye. It's an even bigger shock as it's one of the youngest members of the group who takes such an initiative.

Tauber turns around, 'Yes?'

In an uncertain voice, Hélène tells him that her best friend is in the camp, asking him to assign her to a more protected job. Tauber mutters that he'll see about it, and then leaves.

Afterwards, Tauber assigns Ida to the garment sorting *Kommando* in *Kanada*. Long after the incident, Hélène still doesn't know how to explain why Tauber didn't strike her for speaking out, let alone say why he responded favourably to her request. She's just happy that she did something to improve the lot of a friend.

Chapter 6

Alma

Paris/Brussels, winter 1996-97

From my first contact with Violette and Hélène, Alma Rosé's personality as it appeared in their stories fascinates me. I still don't know if it's the tragedy she experienced in Birkenau, or the protection she offered to all the women in the orchestra – some kind of alma mater? –, which touched me so much. The elegance and dignity of her attitude, not just in her inevitable contact with the Nazis but in everyday life, her human and artistic qualities, her polish and sophistication that

Alma Rosé.

allowed women like Hilde or Anita to have enriching conversations with her, it's all evident whenever anyone talks about her. Except in Fania's book, for which none of the survivors forgave her. Yet her qualities don't fully explain the fascination she exerts, and I've had personal experience of this: no one is indifferent when it comes to Alma. For me, she's a little spark, a glimmer in the barbarism of Birkenau.

When she arrives at the camp, she suddenly finds herself the conductor of this motley group that had previously been led by Tchaïkowska. It's as if a real transmutation was taking place within her: Birkenau wouldn't claim her; she wouldn't allow herself to be its victim. On the contrary, the external reality would have to bend to what she decided it was going to be. Her permanent battle, her rage, to achieve perfection in performing pieces of music seems quite futile when one considers that the orchestra's Block was less than 100 metres from the ramp where the selections were made, where all of the musicians could see what was happening through the window. But by stubbornly bringing them back to their scores, and by concentrating on those little musical notes, Alma was forcing them to momentarily expel the spectacle of everyday horror.

Alma Rosé, conductor of popular music – even at the time, Viennese music wasn't what one could consider as "serious" music –, seems to take on another role under the pressure of the circumstances, that of the soul of the group.

A photograph of her, which appeared in a booklet written by Flora in Dutch, makes me stop. Probably taken when Alma was in her twenties, it painfully captures her eternal youth and, at the same time, the irreparable nature of the loss it symbolizes: among all these deaths that Alma was a part of, among the descendants they never had, how many artists, writers, doctors are there? How many representations of the world will we never enjoy?

*   *   *

Without even realizing it, my encounter with Alma upset me so much that I quickly decide to make her, as well as my search for you, the backbone of this whole story. But as I try to find out more about her, the extent of her character has meant I look less for you: as Sylvia says, you were one of what she calls "the orchestra's little soldiers". Hélène is sure that you would've remained "tied to her apron strings" after your release in order to build on Alma's dream – thus revealing that she did, indeed, dream – of establishing the nucleus of a real orchestra. And I find myself imagining what your life could've been like, if only…

Maybe you would've continued to make music, staying with Alma and following her on tour around the world? Speculations such as this, some more absurd than others, start to develop within me. You wouldn't have gone into exile in Germany, nor gone to the United States, either. You wouldn't have had any children. Would this new orchestra have played in your camp uniform? Would your Birkenau past have followed you, pursued you in your travels? Would you have been considered "the orchestra of former deportees"?

*   *   *

The niece of Gustav Mahler through her mother, herself a converted Jew, Alma was half-Jewish through her father, the famous violinist Arnold Rosé. Until the Nazis came to power, her Jewishness didn't concern her too much, certainly less so than being either a "good" or "bad" musician. She formed a women's orchestra, *Die Wiener Walzermädeln* (the Waltzing Girls of Vienna), with which she toured extensively in Europe, and which specialized in the Viennese Waltz. For a time she was married to a Czech violinist, Vasà Prihoda, with whom she had performed selected violin pieces from the classical repertoire. It was often said that between the two of them, it was Alma who played like a man.

According to Hélène, this de facto competition between two talented artists had an unexpected, but quite logical, conclusion following the eruption of Nazism: those "enlightened" music lovers, musicologists and other hangers on who swarmed around the artists of the time, quickly made Prihoda understand that a Jewish wife could constitute an insurmountable obstacle in the progression of his career, given the situation and the "new" times that were fast approaching. He just needed to be offered an important position as the director of an orchestra, as long as he managed the situation carefully. Having considered his options, Prihoda did the right thing and put an end to the marriage and the musical duo he'd formed with Alma. Having moved to Holland and marrying a Dutch engineer, Alma took refuge in France in 1939. Arrested in 1943, she was transferred to Drancy, then to Auschwitz-I, on 20 July that same year.

*   *   *

I have three photographs of Alma from different times in her life. The first must date from the end of the 1920s and is taken in front of a grey background, with Alma's face, right hand, and the head of a violin illuminated as she holds her finger on the E string. She has a "Charleston" hairstyle, swept over on the right side of her forehead, a round, full face, a rather strong nose, and deliberate and neat chin. It's a face that still has a little of the adolescent about it. The eyes are half-closed, a little sad, almost dead. Only a thin smile assures me that she can't know anything about the drama that awaits her.

A second photograph, clearly taken later as Alma looks noticeably more mature, seems to have come from a Busby Berkeley film, or one of those musical costume comedies that the UFA[10] produced in large quantities in the 1930s. It's taken in Italy, with Alma standing on a stage playing her violin, a curtain forming the backdrop. Her hair is longer and, despite the pose, her body seems supple. She's slightly arched, and is smiling more openly: you can see that she has a dimple on her cheek. In a skilful composition, she's surrounded by musicians from her Viennese ensemble, violinists, a cellist, a harpist and two pianists. The other musicians are all seated, their white dresses flaring out in waves at their feet. Their bodies point towards Alma, but they're looking elsewhere, to the

---

10. *Universum-Film Akiengesellschaft* (UFA), a German film and television company founded in 1917.

left of the stage. With the harp behind her, Alma appears to be almost the ornamental figure. It's undoubtedly a photograph taken for a poster, but not necessarily done in the best taste.

The third image is from a newspaper clipping. Alma is visiting her father, Arnold Rosé. Her dark hair is pulled back slightly and she's wearing a white striped dress. Her face is thinner, with a vague smile. Although she may not have had time to strike a pose, she still looks serene.

When she arrived at Auschwitz, Alma was 37 years old. Every testimony about her mentions that she wasn't extraordinarily beautiful, and that her face only had regular features, but she was striking due to the intensity of her gaze, her demeanour, and the elegance of her movements. Her hands were those of an artist's, with long fingers.

She had adopted a particular gait very early in her life in an attempt to hide the fact that she had a slight hip defect. As a result, she walked slowly and only took small steps. Her limp was noticeable when she had to move quicker, particularly when she had to get off her podium after finishing the concerts at the gates or in the "sauna" on Sunday afternoons.

Her descent into hell hadn't broken her, and she always kept her dignified bearing and posture. Only a few white hairs mixed in with the brown might have suggested a difficult life. Having not really experienced any deprivations before her arrest, she was still in relatively good health, which made her a "subject of choice" for Dr Carl Clauberg's gynaecological experiments in Block No. 10 at Auschwitz-I.

To help ensure the Nazi's ultimate control of the world, Clauberg was looking for the fastest and most economical way for the mass sterilisation of Jews. He used the most sophisticated, wildest and most absurd methods, including performing X-rays at high doses, multiple injections of solutions which burned and killed his "patients", and injections of the most bizarre decoctions, all on the orders and under the supervision of Himmler himself. Alma would never tell anyone about the abominations she witnessed in the Block.

Having been recognized by an inmate before being selected by Clauberg, she would have to prove her violinist skills to the head of Block 10, on his birthday. He immediately transferred her to Birkenau, where Hössler gave her the role of orchestra conductor, replacing Tchaïkowska, who was then promoted to *Blockälteste*.

*   *   *

Birkenau, spring 1944

The incessant chatter in the middle of a concert by two *Aufseherinen* is starting to become annoying. Irritated, Alma has already turned around several times to stare at them intensely. It's a look the girls in the orchestra know well, and it's never a good sign when she glares at them like that. They know it means a brief shouting match awaits them, accompanied by some form of punishment such as extra rehearsals in the evening after their meal, or washing the music room floor. It's exactly what happened to Anita after she returned from the *Revier* following typhus. Still very weak, she was unable to see or hear very well and so played several wrong notes and couldn't seem to find the correct beat. Refusing to take her condition into account – the show must go on, after all – Alma forced her to wash the floor for a week.

However, the two Nazis don't react to Alma's glare and continue to chat. Alma rolls her eyes and whispers, 'It can't go on like this anymore…' Then with a gesture, she stops everyone and turns around. More of a *grande dame* than ever before, she assumes her haughty *Kapellmeister* voice and calls out to them from the top of her podium: 'Please stop talking; you're hindering the flow of the concert.'

The two SS guards stop, astonished. 'The music doesn't start again until you shut up,' declares Alma. The subjugated supervisors are finally silenced, and the concert resumes. The girls look at each other, amazed. 'What a woman, eh?'

For Alma, there's little to be triumphant about, even if her attitude towards the Nazis appears to be either one of heroism or recklessness. She cares deeply about what she does and these Sunday afternoon concerts are important to all of the inmates, including her. They provide a little extra hope and a nostalgic reminder of what life was like before all this. Nothing can or should take precedence over music, in Birkenau just as everywhere else.

*   *   *

Alma is vigilant with the women in her orchestra and is constantly on the lookout for signs of collapse, nervous breakdown, moral and physical carelessness etc. However, she's also looking for negligence when performing the pieces, anything, indeed, that's likely to threaten the organisation she's building is immediately put down. Frau Kroner is regularly yelled at because she often dozes a little between movements; something that still makes Sylvia laugh when she thinks about it many years later.

With a desperate energy, Alma strives by herself to build a fantasy of peace and tranquillity in the electrified walls of Birkenau, where the chimneys of the crematoria and the pyres that smoke continuously are only 100 metres away. By making them play their instruments relentlessly, perhaps she hopes she can somehow protect the women from the ugliness and bloodshed, forcing them to think of nothing other than the music. She requires their constant attention and full commitment when playing. Having a particularly keen ear, she can hear where the wrong notes and chords are coming from. Then she tirelessly starts the piece again and, potentially, punishes the culprits if they play below the standards she's set for them: after playing a wrong note, Violette has to clean the music room floor by hand for a week. Yvette, who after one time entering at the wrong moment during a passage in *Madame Butterfly*, finds the conductor's baton in her face so many times that, terrified by Alma's anger, she has to rely on Lily to signal to her when to come in.

As for you, Elsa, the wise, sweet Elsa, you've also been punished a few times. Although a fairly good technician, you still have sudden bursts of passive resistance against Alma's authoritarianism. She brings back family memories that still gnaw you and as a result, you (almost) intentionally play wrong notes just to see Alma get angry. Forced to rehearse again in the evening when the whole orchestra has finished its work, you dejectedly play your part with Zosha, exchanging smiles and sighs while strumming your violins. Yes, Alma is dignified and even manages to impose her respectability on the Nazis, but she can be a nightmare when you don't do what she asks!

Alma is completely convinced by the idea that the only way to fight against violence from the outside is to put it aside in a proactive way, by imposing another discipline on top of it, one that's almost as strict, but based on other values. In the orchestra Block, it's not Nazi order that must dominate, but something of a different calibre, which emanates from one's own person and inner vision, the distinction, and harmony of the music. It's a little pathetic, but it does sometimes work, especially with Hélène. These two women, with very different social backgrounds, ages and experiences, communicate through music. Hélène is enriched immeasurably through her contact with Alma, who is able to make her understand and soften the often stiff rhythm of a waltz by comparing it to a bouncing ball.

Hélène agrees to enter into Alma's vision and in return, at rare moments, it allows her to withdraw from their reality and flee into these worlds evoked by the music, to feel the wind on her face, hear the birds in the trees and the gallop of a horse in the forest... She sometimes thinks to herself that she's lucky to have this means of escape, and pities those who, by not entering into the "game", are forced to remain permanently in hell.

Hélène remembers that from time to time during rehearsals, when she wasn't satisfied with the ensemble, Alma would point to the crematoria and say: 'That's what awaits us if we're not able to play well. The Germans don't care about a mediocre orchestra. We need to be as good and as well-rehearsed as if we were playing a concert at Madison Square Garden!'

Alma certainly isn't self-indulgent and after the day's rehearsal with the orchestra, she locks herself in the small room that serves as her bedroom. The Nazis have given her permission to keep the light on and even have a window so as to be better lit during her solitary work. She tirelessly repeats her solos and contributions in the orchestral parts and once she's fairly satisfied with her endeavours, she works late into the night orchestrating arrangements to suit the group's particular sound. She finds new harmonies to compensate for the lack of wind instruments and the weakness in the basses: Yvette has progressed well on the double bass and there's been a cello since November following the arrival of Anita, but it still doesn't generate the sound of a symphony orchestra.

Alma has to use all her know-how and sensitivity as a musician to orchestrate pieces of music for which, most of the time, she's only able to obtain the piano score from the camp authorities. Sometimes she even has to search her memory to find pieces she's played before in order to expand their repertoire. Fania's arrival in January 1944 has been a great help to her as she has a prodigious memory and knows the scores and arrangements for many musical works. Since then, Alma has relied heavily on Fania to make what they play as diverse as possible.

Their repertoire now includes more than 150 different titles, including current hits such as arias by Peter Kreuder and Zara

Leander; light music; Viennese waltzes; operetta excerpts by Franz Lehar, as well as more imposing pieces from the classical repertoire such as Brahms, Weber, Verdi, and even passages from Dvoràk's *New World Symphony*, which has been put together in a sort of medley called *Dvoràkianna*. Every time they play it with Alma, the girls have a tiny but delicious sense of misbehaving: 'How stupid are these Nazis?!' They also play minor works, but ones that still require virtuosity, including Monti's *Csárdás* and Sarasate's *Zigeunerweisen*, with Alma naturally providing the solos.

Then there's the inevitable nightmare of having to chain together military marches during the departure and return of the *Aussenkommandos*; key moments of the day when the women of the orchestra see all the "able-bodied" personnel of the camp parading in front of them as they march off to the arms factories or to road and railway construction sites.

It's a genuine triumph that Alma has managed to unite this disparate ensemble and make the military marches convincing, "catchy" and martial, just as the Nazis want them to be. It certainly takes a musical ear and plenty of creativity to make accordions and mandolins sound like trumpets and trombones!

Intelligent and energetic, Alma quickly leads the orchestra to a very special status in the camp. As far as the lower-ranking SS guards and members of the camp's small hierarchy are concerned, the musicians are merely parasites to be sent immediately to the oven. Yet for the senior executives, Hössler, then Kramer, Mandl, Mengele, and Tauber, the orchestra is becoming increasingly indispensable. They're almost proud to have a group led by a prestigious artist performing in front of visitors from other camps, or from the *Lager* headquarters in Berlin. Indeed, it's said that even Himmler would've seen Alma play...

*   *   *

This change of status brings with it many advantages. Alma is able to speak almost on an equal footing with the SS, and has virtually complete control over the organisation of the orchestra, its repertoire, and the recruitment of new female musicians. She even dismissed a few girls after her arrival as she believed them to be too weak technically and musically. Three of them are now *Stubendienst* in the orchestra's Block, but Alma was unable to help another girl who instead has been transferred to a "normal" working *Kommando* in *Kanada*. Alma had to report to Maria Mandl about any Polish and non-Jewish girls who were "dismissed", as she didn't want the orchestra to be made up exclusively of Jewish musicians. Insisting that every dismissal be submitted to her, Alma simply replied '*zu befehl*', ('as you command'), turned her back, and left. Since then, she's only had one point of disagreement with the *Oberaufseherin* concerning two singers, one Polish, the other Jewish. Mandl decided that only the non-Jewish singer would be included, meaning the superb voice of the other singer wasn't enough to save her.

On a similar occasion, Alma also chose Fania, a cabaret artist, to the detriment of another inmate with the voice of an opera singer, as she felt she needed to diversify the repertoire as much as possible and no longer limit herself to classical music. Fania brought that spark of colour variety singers have that the other woman didn't.

Since her arrival, the orchestra's size has grown from less than twenty to over forty, including copyists. In the beginning, everything came from the orchestra in the men's camp, but Alma quickly obtained better instruments, and even received a precious violin from Mandl, which was no doubt stolen from a deportee.

The material benefits she's able to obtain for the girls are substantial, especially food supplements. She can ask Mandl for a double ration of bread, for example, which is a basic currency in the camp that's used to gain a favour or a scarce commodity, such as soap. However, Alma considers this double ration to be a reward, not a right. When she says, 'Today you played like pigs!' the girls know what it means: no extra food. Zosha remembers that she was also granted access to the camp's book depot, and the subsequent atmosphere in the Block was quickly transformed.

As an added advantage, the girls are entitled to a daily hot shower in the "sauna". In the hotbed of infection and overcrowding that is the camp, the ability to stay fairly clean and wash your clothes is no guarantee of survival, but it does provide an additional chance to fight chronic epidemics. Alma makes sure everyone takes a shower, and punishes those who refuse. Lili, often reluctant to emerge wet into the cold Polish winter, suffers the consequences from Alma. She also makes sure that everyone gets into the habit of examining their hair. After all, lice are dangerous because they carry all of Birkenau's curses, especially typhus.

As the surrounding area is swampy, the Block is laid out to protect the instruments from humidity. The floor was laid down by inmates from the carpentry *Kommando*, and a stove installed in the music room. Indeed, the Block is the only one out of all the buildings housing inmates that wasn't built with a dirt or cracked-cement floor, which would have been severely abrasive for the instruments. What's more, on the pretext that musicians can't play if they have frostbite, they're spared the endless rollcalls that exhaust their less-privileged comrades: an *Aufseherin* lines them up in the morning before going out, then counts them in the evening after they've played at the gate, and that's it for the day.

Driven by Alma, the orchestra's standard rises dramatically. She clearly explains what she wants to hear, occasionally using her violin to demonstrate phrasing and nuance, but above all, she never forgives any musical mistakes and continues to demand more and more from her musicians. The rehearsals lengthen, with the girls often playing music for more than eight hours a day, but their hard work pays off. In this hellish place, which is an insult to mankind, some of the musicians even find themselves forgetting, if only for a brief moment, where they are, as they play and play again.

Even if not everyone likes Alma (after all, you, Elsa, Anita and Violette don't really appreciate her bossy and perfectionist side. A little too Germanic, perhaps?), everyone is seduced by her personality. They know how much she clings to her music so as not to sink into a fatal depression, and understand the fierce discipline she imposes on herself to block out those things that make up the very essence of Birkenau: annihilation, industrial murder, and the destruction of mankind.

*   *   *

In a rare moment of abandonment, Alma confides in a friend, Margarete, an Austrian like herself, that she doesn't really understand what's going on. She's built a fragile barrier inside of her so as to prevent the outside world, one delimited by barbed wire and watchtowers, from completely taking over, only keeping it in place thanks to a sole gigantic effort of willpower. Nevertheless, she asks Margarete how it is that the whole world lets them die here without intervening.

This refusal to be twisted and broken by the Nazi machine doesn't mean that she isn't aware of her surroundings. One evening during *Lagersperre* [quarantine], when inmates are strictly forbidden to leave the Blocks, she slips into the shadows outside. Everyone in the camp knows what *Lagersperre* means: there will have been a "selection" at the *Revier*, and the chosen women will be taken by truck to the gas chamber, after having spent one or more nights without eating or drinking in the "antechamber of death", Block 25. Unlike those sent to their death from the train ramp, these women know what fate awaits them. Mad with anguish, despair or helpless anger, they scream incessantly as the trucks take them to the other end of the camp, to the last stop, the concrete buildings, the site of their murder. As a final insult to the condemned, before entering Block 25 the SS strip them naked so that they don't have to do it once they're dead.

Leaning against the wall of the Block, Alma hears the women scream and sticks her fingers in her ears, whispering: 'I hope I don't have to die like this...' She starts to cry.

Zofia Cykowiak witnesses the same scene, and would later describe it to me as Alma's moment of weakness. She takes her in her arms, without saying a word, and calms her by rocking her a little, before walking away discreetly to allow her to regain her composure. Afterwards, when she slips outside during the night, Zofia is careful not to come across Alma, so as not to embarrass her. But since that night, she believes she saw in Alma's eyes a misunderstanding and distress that she still can't speak about without becoming emotional, even fifty years later.

And so, Alma, the Greek statue and heroine of tragedy, also had her moment of despair. It's this moment that makes her dear to me. It humanizes her, feminizes her, and somewhat tempers the image of perfectionism attributed to her in the memories of all the survivors. Alma not only seduces me as an artist thrown into the abyss by Nazism, but also as a woman, in her strength as well as in her fragility. See, these are the same terms as when I talk about you. What a coincidence...

Chapter 7

Hairdresser and Beauty Salon:
"Paris-Beauté"

Cologne, December 1996

I've wanted to go to Cologne for several weeks. Your friend Ruth is ready to welcome and spend some time with me, and I really want to revisit various places again: the salon; your house; the Ring, that boulevard that surrounds the city and which I used to walk along in all directions just to kill time when you lived there, and when you had so little time for me.

During the journey there and back on the train I'm in some discomfort. I have palpitations, the classic symptoms of a heart attack, which I can only get rid of with my new crutch; the anxiolytics [anti-anxiety drugs]. The anguish I feel is, of course, for Germany, the train, and your absence renewed again. But suddenly I understand. It's exactly forty years since I came to see you for the first time in Cologne, where you were living in exile, during the 1956 winter holidays. Forty years. The same age you were when you died. A funny kind of birthday. In my mind there are no longer any coincidences, everything has a meaning directly linked to our common history. I remember what I worried about back then, that you wouldn't be there when I arrived, that I might miss you altogether; a worry I tried to dispel by asking the conductor in very rudimentary German what time we would arrive. I can still see the number 4711 – the Eau de Cologne brand famous for its bergamot scent – written in blue-green neon numbers in an ellipse at the entrance to the station.

I already know that I won't find much of the city I knew before. After all, it's been rebuilt over and over again. As soon as I arrive, I start to walk around the centre and the cathedral. Everything is strangely familiar to me, but on a different scale: Cologne really is the city of my childhood. Hardly anything remains of the horrid nineteenth-century red-black brick houses that I used to know. Bland buildings from the 70s and 80s, made of concrete and glass, have replaced them. There are some futuristic buildings too, beautiful and sharp, like the headquarters of the savings bank which I stand in front of for half an hour to take stock and dream.

It's a week before Christmas, and the atmosphere is frenzied, just like it is everywhere. The whole population seems to have gathered in this part of the city where the department stores, luxury boutiques and trendy cafes are. For the first time I notice people jostling and making no effort to avoid each other, and never saying 'sorry' when they bump into one another. I want to warm up a bit, but when I enter a store and hold the door to the person following me, they look at me like I'm from Mars, before thanking me. What happened to that refinement? That proverbial shared politeness by all Germans that gave me shivers down my spine when I was little? In a completely irrational way, I look around the crowd as if to spot familiar faces.

The "Paris-Beauté" salon no longer exists, having been replaced by a travel agency. Is this ironic or just a sign of things moving on? The "UFA Palast", the cinema on the corner, is still there. I used to go there often during the day, particularly when the atmosphere in the salon was too much for me, to watch inane, sentimental, syrupy German comedies from the 1960s.

As I pass this myriad of places, I conscientiously make an inventory of each one. I also look for the "Rudi Rau" restaurant where we would go from time to time at noon, when your work allowed, but it's no longer there. I take a walk in the park in front of your house, where I played football by myself. I used to do archery there, too, and once almost accidentally killed a little girl with an arrow. The memory still makes me shudder today.

The park is pretty bare, and the few bald trees and sparse grass make me completely depressed.

*   *   *

Ruth greets me at her house. Just like the last time, in 1964, I'm to sleep in her son Danny's room, and I once again take stock of all the time that has passed, and what has changed. The first time I was here I was staying in a little boy's room, but now I'm in a man's room, surrounded by the memories of his childhood, his academic achievements, his teenage years, his travels, and his hobbies. I see myself in this room, learning my first guitar chords, dreaming of your impossible death. I start to bathe in an ocean of self-compassion, and shake myself to get out of it as quickly as possible.

Ruth tells me about your friendship, which began a few days after her marriage here, in the winter of 1956, and of the rare confidences you revealed to her about your past, and your life that had been shattered over and over again.

You'd obviously known for a long time that it was impossible to talk to people about Birkenau. It wasn't comprehensible to anyone who hadn't been there or, more simply, such an outrageous reality was just too complicated to put into words. You'd told her something about it, however, in very general terms, because she had an ability to listen that you might never have experienced before. After all, she was your friend. I learn through Ruth that you hadn't really liked Alma, whose face and character now haunt me more and more. You disliked her perfectionism and authoritarian side. At the time, of course, you couldn't perceive what an impact this would have on you, and which would affect me enormously.

Thanks to Ruth, I understand the importance that the *Chaconne* had for you, how it linked you to Hélène, how you intervened on her behalf to get her an audition. But above all, I gain some insight into your day-to-day life in Cologne, your overwhelming desire to start from scratch and then your disillusionment, not to mention your sudden, quasi-brutal departure for the United States.

Ruth confessed to me that she was angry with you for leaving me so far behind ... and I envied her a little for allowing herself to feel that, me who never stopped wondering if I hadn't chased you away by not loving you enough myself. Eager to make sense of it all, I suddenly tell myself that you might have wanted to go, leaving everything behind you, without erasing your tracks, but without worrying about having left any behind; those living traces, such as myself, then the more intangible ones such photographs and memories left behind the gaze and recollections of others. These traces which become blurred and gradually fade, until people say: 'Well, in the end, we didn't really know her ...' And then I remember that the last record you bought in Cologne was *Non, je ne regrette rien* by that other "sparrow", Édith Piaf.

You left behind a violin with Ruth, a poor violin without a bow, without a case, without even a bridge or trigger guard, just a simple shell; a representation of yourself, perhaps? Meaning well, she wants to give it to me as a remembrance of you. Admittedly, I don't have any material memories of you, except for a few pictures. But knowing that you gave it to her, I see no reason to take it; it's perfect where it is.

Ruth also remembers a particularly memorable visit in 1960: Renate, Anita's sister, had come to see you and given you a nice photograph of her, with a loving dedication: 'For Elsa, in memory of the good... and the bad days.' At the back of the salon, Renate had noticed a horrible child, flighty and badly put together. That was me, in the gynaeceum.[11] Thirty-five years later, Anita still

---

11. A building or portion of a house in Ancient Greece that was reserved solely for women.

remembers the bad impression I had left on her sister, and tells me about it, half-laughing.

Ruth finally tells me about a very strange episode, which took place sometime after your death. She answered the door, and it was my mother! My grandmother was standing there in front of her, dressed in your clothes, your coat, with one of your handbags, all objects that Ruth knew very well. I don't know the purpose of my grandmother's visit, and Ruth can't remember either. But I can see the caricature in my mind and I laugh with it, overwhelmed, angry and helpless. As symbolic as the gesture is, I don't fully understand it, and I don't really want to look for any meaning in it. Was it to try to replace you, to show the magnitude of her loss, to appropriate all that remains of you, to make you live again after the irreparable damage that had been caused? Who knows?

*   *   *

Setting off on a pilgrimage to try to find traces of you, to walk once again in your footsteps and in mine, I still think about my cumbersome grandmother as I go on my way. Whatever happened, isn't she still a part of your history?

I now think I was looking for confirmation from your friend of a hunch that I'd had for a long time: you were never able to lead a life where events articulated themselves into something vaguely continuous. Accidents, break-ups, they happen in everyone's life. But you, you'd only known departures, ruptures, escapes, breakdowns and abandonment, one after the other. Each new episode seemed designed to give you a new chance to exist, to live your life differently, on the sole condition that it cost you everything you had. What a waste.

For some time I've wondered about the part that we, your relatives, played in your last avatar. Had we locked you into your image of a former deportee? Had we made you an eternal outcast?

Is that why you left? Did you want to abandon Europe for good, and rid yourself of the memories and those striped images of Birkenau and Belsen you no longer wanted to carry with you? This hope of a new life in a different place that was completely unknown to you, did you have to pay for it by leaving behind all that you loved? Me, your family, your friends?

I now find I'm telling myself that this search for you I undertook a year ago doesn't necessarily have to be a Greek tragedy anymore. At first I'm a little empty and sad in Cologne, depressed by the festive atmosphere sustained with lanterns, foliage on storefronts, Bavarian oompah-pah music, and impulsive shoppers, which can be seen everywhere at Christmas time. I'm also sad because it had basically been agreed that I had to be like this, as was always the case where you were concerned.

I force myself to walk around the city in all directions. It's freezing cold and I'm hungry because I'm delaying going into a restaurant as much as possible. It's as if I can only associate you with the suffering and physical misery that I foolishly try to imitate for myself.

I'm also sad at the obvious, logical observation that there was no trace of you in the city. What was I looking for? A monument? A marble plaque attached to the salon building at Habsburgerring 18/20, or to your house at Rathenauplatz 1? Some mourners perhaps, assembled around me like an ancient choir, to sing of my suffering as an orphan approaching his fifties, my madness as an angry teenager, or my childish incomprehension?

I can also now see the good times we had more clearly, how your wavy hair used to move; it was auburn, although I once said you were a redhead and you said 'No! It's mahogany', which made me laugh. I see you laughing again, with that particular way you had of throwing your head back when you did so, your sparkling eyes and your teeth that stuck out a little, and your way of singing Charles Trenet's *Le Soleil a rendez-vous avec la lune*, and how you used to change the lyrics.

I see us shopping together, I see you cooking – you were a good cook – and I remember our moments of intimacy, when you washed my hair and your hands lingered there, taking care that the shampoo didn't sting my eyes. And those packages you sent when I was at summer camp, full of the sweets and pretzels that I loved, which proved to me that you didn't ignore the things I cherished. Did you make them thinking that you would have liked to receive such things at some point?

I hear you ask, 'how much do you love me?' and I always answered '112 percent!' I'd started saying that to you when I was about 6 years old, when the mathematical notion of "infinity" was still unknown to me and that was the highest number I knew. It always made you laugh. I can also see some of the photographs taken over forty years ago, where we are together, in bed, where I have to admit that you were completely there with me, and that in the end, it wasn't a former deportee who'd been almost entirely destroyed by her ordeals that was next to me, but simply – forgive me for saying "simply" – my attentive mother, listening to her little boy tell her that, the day before, he'd seen a ladybird.

I immerse myself in this constant unhappiness of your story, almost to the point of successfully cutting myself off from all that was kind, joyful, funny and carefree about you. However, I start telling myself that maybe there was something else deep inside you besides submission, something strong and supple like silk, which meant you could bow to the inevitable, but would never actually break. What was it that kept you calm and serene in Birkenau, and then helped you overcome those hardships deemed insurmountable for a woman: a failed marriage, the separation from her child, cascading losses and sorrows? There was something there that always made you return stubbornly to the fight, my valiant little mother of whom I can finally be proud. Yes, I'm starting to admire you once more, instead of feeling that humiliating pity that's been eating away at me for years.

Paris, 1 January 1997
We're having dinner at a restaurant in Montparnasse with a friend of Violette's, Anne-Lise. As we talk about their daily life in the camp, I realize that it's not that out of place to talk about hunger and death while eating a plate of meat covered in sauce. The thought surprises me. What's happening? Any hesitation I have that seems to prevail when I talk about these things seems out of place with these two women. We talk about their showers, the daily showers the girls in the orchestra have, as well as the monthly showers of those unfortunate women who suffer a common fate.

All of a sudden, Violette starts. She tells me, a little shaken, that she's just had a vision of you again in the shower over there, a white silhouette under the water, with that fair-haired milky white skin that you gave me – and that I never really thanked you for. Anne-Lise, in her turn, can feel the impression of their clothing's rough fabric on her fingertips after they've been disinfected and steamed following their shower. It's a strange sensation, not particularly unpleasant, of a material neither completely dry nor completely wet, just soaked in steam.

I'm touched by these two recollections. Through their psychic acts, these two women have helped guide me through the process I've been undertaking. I can see you through Violette's eyes in that shower, washing yourself conscientiously like you do everything else, knowing that in addition to the pleasure of being clean, you were protecting your very existence by getting rid of – if only for a short time – something of the stain, of the stench of Birkenau.

Violette will often tell me about you. She talks of your mixture of fragility and firmness that I knew well, about your childish and mischievous smile. That way you had of reassuring others by your presence or actions when those frictions, those small jealousies that were inevitable in such a disparate group, caused conflicts to arise. I see you once more trying to iron out those difficulties and misunderstandings in our family ten years later, and in the end I see that you hadn't changed; the disagreements around you still made you uncomfortable.

Chapter 8

Second Violin

I arrive at a really bad time. On the day I get there, King Hussein is making a formal apology to the families of children killed whilst on a bus at the border, after a Jordanian soldier sprayed the vehicle with a submachine gun. The country is traumatized, as most places are after the same kind of ordeal, especially when children are concerned. In addition, the government has decided to establish a new housing development in the eastern part of Jerusalem – a settlement, as they say here. People fear a new wave of attacks. There are armed soldiers everywhere and the atmosphere is far from peaceful.

In Amsterdam, my transit airport, I'm used to how things work: fastidious checks, innocently stupid questions such as: 'Why are you going through Amsterdam to go to Tel Aviv?' Answer: 'Because KLM had a sale on and those were the terms…' Question: 'Yes, but why Amsterdam…?' etc. I'm dressed entirely in black leather, which I presume probably corresponds to their composite portrait of a bomber or drug dealer.

I'd written to Regina Küpferberg, Hilde and Sylvia around ten days earlier to tell them about my intended visit, and had left as soon as possible, without waiting for a response; I know from Violette that the average response time for a letter addressed to Hilde is three years.

I'd already visited Israel as a tourist in the summer of 1958. Back then, I'd found the people to be rather rude, or "badly brought up", like they say about a child who pushes you around without saying sorry, or someone who asks you for the time or for some directions, then never thanks you for the information. No doubt the prerogative of a new and young society.

A French friend who I'm staying with for a few days tells me how he had to unlearn how to say: 'sorry, please, thank you, hello etc.', all these little niceties we use to help those relationships we're obliged to have throughout our lives with strangers, whether in the street, on the train, or in a restaurant. Now when my friend wants get to off a train he has to punch and kick his way through the crowd when he reaches his destination. Those little enclaves of personal space that are tacitly respected in older, Western societies are lacking here. Aside from this roughness in social relationships, the complexity of Israeli society is immediately noticeable, and for anyone on the outside – and who wishes to remain so – it's quite exciting.

* * *

Right off the bat, I ask myself what language I should use with Sylvia and Hilde: German? Hebrew? I can easily imagine that Hilde and her husband speak to each other in German, but what effect might that language have on them if used by a third party? When in doubt, I opt for Hebrew.

Accompanied by my interpreter, I telephone the three women I came to see. Things begin badly: none of them has received the letter I sent announcing my visit. Sylvia won't be able to see me on this occasion: her son is getting married and it's apparently more a chore for her than anything else, as the son in question has "returned to religion" and so wears a kippah and has curls, eats kosher food etc. Apparently, he's become a boring fanatic. Through my interpreter, I tell Sylvia that I'm writing a book about her life and that of her friends in the orchestra. She laughs at this and admits that her life could be the subject of several books. There's a liveliness in her voice, a humour too, and she agrees to help me, a little later, once the marriage is settled. We arrange another date in a few weeks' time and I wish her 'Mazel Tov' (good luck) for the wedding, to which she laughs even more and says her goodbyes.

Meanwhile, Regina's husband is having heart trouble and she's currently unable to meet me due to his health concerns. Hilde is also unavailable: her daughter-in-law is in labour and there are complications with the birth. As a result, she has to take care of her grandchildren and can't devote much time to me, although she does say that she can meet me at some point during the week that I'm here. Hilde freely informs me that my arrival into their lives has given rise to volleys of phone calls between all three women. They're intrigued by my project, perhaps even worried by it.

Netzer Sereni,[12] *March 1997*
After several unsuccessful attempts to meet them, Hilde has finally agreed to meet me one morning. Much to my chagrin, she doesn't remember you at all as she welcomes me into her home on the kibbutz, one of the largest and richest in Israel, or at least it was until the economic crises hit hard in the early 1980s. After the meal, it takes us almost an hour to visit just a small part of it, including the bomb shelters, the watchtower, the memorial to the Shoah victims, the small vault under the library containing the six metal candlesticks representing the "six million victims", as well as the ledger in which each person of the kibbutz could write down their history and the names of missing family members. There are flowers everywhere, as well as a few gigantic palm trees, hundreds of years old, not to mention trees, fruits, other greenery, animals; it's a farmer's paradise.

---

12. A collective community founded in 1948 by Holocaust survivors who were liberated from Buchenwald.

Hilde lives in a tiny apartment just the way I like them; full of books and music. Sitting around the table with her and her husband, we talk about my project. I try to explain through my interpreter what I want to do, and what I'm not going to do. We spend some time trying to conjure up your face but, despite the picture I show to Hilde, she still isn't able to recollect you. In desperation, I hide the lower part of my face, leaving only my forehead on show, as I believe that's the part of me that most resembles my mother. Nothing works. Back in Auschwitz, you ate at the same table as Carla, Sylvia, and Ruth, the "German-speaking band", but you were the link, the hinge with the French and Belgian group! Not anymore.

I finally realize that it's no wonder she's forgotten about you. If you had a designated function in that group, beyond your place at the second violin desk, it was to smooth out the rough edges and erase any conflicts. You weren't one of those people everyone remembers for their energy and loud mouth, like Violette, or for their talent as a musician, like Big Hélène. From what I know about you, it was your discretion and concern not to cut corners or to clash with the others that prevailed the most.

After completing the tour of the kibbutz, Hilde and Regina have to leave for work as they are on duty that afternoon. Hilde walks back to the car with us before hurrying off, turning briefly for a moment to wave us goodbye. There's a little lump in my throat as I watch her walk away, dressed in her purple jacket and navy blue trousers, a dignified little figure and a great lady.

* * *

I now know that when I went looking for them, your former colleagues, it was mostly the sound of your name in their mouths that I was looking for, the clarification I needed. Yet I was both blind and deaf to what was going on inside me, this abstract desire to understand, and the anger and frustration I felt at your supposed inability to fight, both for you and, incidentally, for me. This is the reason why I often missed any mention of you in their stories. It was almost the same as when you were alive; we always seemed to just pass by each other without ever really connecting. That's why it didn't hurt me to admit that Hilde, Regina, Sylvia, and Yvette had forgotten you. As I couldn't "see" you, it was natural to me simply to accept that you'd been erased, or for want of a better word, forgotten. Anytime those that did remember talked about you – always for the good – it didn't really upset me. Was this because I wanted to keep this image of a submissive and non-existent woman and mother at all costs? Or was it, on the contrary, that what they told me wasn't a surprise, as it resonated with what I've always known without ever accepting it; that you were more alive, stronger and more determined than what we, your family, were ever willing to credit you with?

In this immediate absence of any emotion, the mystery that your life represents for me had all the room necessary to continue to be so. I could live with this paradox of both longing and refusing to hear the truth about you, instead of the same recurring statements I hated which were constantly repeated by the family, and that I'd even started to repeat myself, against my will. I couldn't ignore it any longer.

In order for everything to remain unbroken inside of me, I had to lock away this image of a silent and inactive mother, who in reality was more alive, more present, less destroyed than I thought. Yet I had to prevent her from resurfacing at any cost, silencing the occasionally violent or negative emotions that this return could provoke. But now this was no longer possible; I'd not found you completely, but I'd finally seen you at the end of the tunnel, and that makes another trip possible, this time one inside myself, which is perhaps even more perilous: I'll be able to look for you inside of me.

Putting myself in your shoes, trying to see what these women told me about their lives as if you were watching them, was a way of using my imagination to take your place. It was what your brother childishly, absurdly, had planned to do when you were arrested, that grim spring of 1943, but which he – luckily for everyone – didn't achieve. However, I don't believe he's ready to forgive himself for having failed.

As your son born in spite of everything, who keeps your voice inside him like an internal whisper, but is no longer able to see your face, by realizing this fantasy fifty years after your release, I almost found the best way to erase you, to lose you forever. And that's what would have happened if I'd followed this process to its logical end, writing a book purely about the orchestra, in which you would've been one of the most non-descript characters, and what would otherwise have no doubt been an Alma-centric book. For a time, fascinated as I was by the dimensions of her character, crushed by her as you all were, I undoubtedly let her occupy your place in my imagination, and I loved her as I would've liked to have loved you while you were alive.

This book, which I'd been planning for a while and was luckily prevented from finishing, would've been the surest way, in the end, to abandon you forever, without recourse, in the yellowish winds of Birkenau.

Netzer Sereni, April 1997

We're in the community dining room and it's quite an emotional moment for me. I knew from the start that Hilde was a Zionist, even before her deportation, and that this kibbutz she'd helped found was almost the fulfilment of an ideal that had helped her through Birkenau and Belsen, and all the hardships she'd experienced before then in a Nazified Germany.

Most of the people eating their lunch in the dining room had gone through similar trials to Hilde – as the numbers tattooed on their left arms testified – and now clung to this ground with their teeth and fingernails to make it their homeland. There was an overwhelming sense of history and experience in this room that was impossible to ignore, and although I hadn't shared these experiences, I can, and will, respect it for the symbolic power it has. One only has to hear how the words *Eretz Yisrael*, the Land of Israel, spoken with affection and sung almost with a fervour, sound in their mouths.

Surrounded by all of these people, we continue to discuss the validity of my project, until the million dollar question arises: 'Who are *you* to tell our story?' However incomplete my answer may be, it seems to reassure her somewhat.

I don't want to interview them collectively, which according to Hilde would be the best way, as I don't want them correcting each other. The parts that they forget or their contradictions with each other's stories interest me as much as what they agree on. I don't have the slightest idea as yet what this book will be like, but I know it won't fall into the same category as Fania's, or worse, the film and play that were based on it. I'm not a historian, just the son of one, and I know that if I don't do them justice, it will hurt your memory too. I can't guarantee Hilde that this project will satisfy all of them, I can only guarantee that I'll be honest. I can't – and certainly don't want – to write under their collective control either, because it's their individual stories that I am looking for, and that I need in order for the book to work.

*   *   *

Hilde leaves to go find Regina and introduce us. It's at this point I realize that, delicately and subtly, she's been putting me through some sort of test. As the three of them don't remember you, and therefore don't recognize me, it may mean they want to give themselves the time and means to work out who I am, and what right I have to share this part of their past with them. If, in the end, they agree to work with me, it won't be because I'm my mother's son, but because my project is likely to suit them.

As it was with Hélène and Violette, when I meet Regina it's once again her voice that strikes me the most. She's already a relatively old woman, and you can tell that her life has been very much about action, creation and struggle, and she appears to be one of those people who, in Israel, had the opportunity to rebuild themselves at the same time as they were building their country, stone by stone. Her hands are chafed, she's started to have difficulty walking, can't see very well, and has to protect her eyes from light. In spite of this she has a vibrant, young, punchy voice that still hints at the explosive energy that drives her. And just as it was with Hilde and her husband Pise, I'm not on a friendly footing quite yet; that would be premature. But it's still an equal relationship and there's a closeness that takes very little time to develop. Is it Israel, the kibbutz, or our personalities which make things easy between us? It matters little.

As we walk, Regina confesses to me in broken English that she suffered for years after the privileged status she occupied in Birkenau, when she was a *Stubendienst* specially engaged to help Alma. She'd been angry at Hilde for years for having been the one responsible for her joining the group. Finally, ill, and believing herself on the verge of death, she was at last able to talk to Hilde about it, and has felt more at peace with herself ever since.

Regina tells me she doesn't remember anything; that she no longer wants to remember anything, and that besides, she was nothing more than a simple orderly, whose story is of no interest. She fears that she's been forgotten by her comrades and, at the same time, worries that she left behind an unflattering image of herself. I don't know what to say to her in reply, except that I'm very interested in her story. She saw Alma from a different perspective than the other girls; being at the centre of the orchestra and the rest of the camp, she was able to see what was going on both inside and outside the Block. She experienced the scandal of music at Auschwitz on a daily basis, this human activity that was carried out almost normally, in what was otherwise generalized madness. It's precisely this position that makes her story fascinating.

Still unconvinced of any interest in what she has to say, she nevertheless agrees to see me the next time I come to Israel. In the end, it would appear my examination has gone rather well, as the three ladies now deem me worthy – or at least capable – of hearing their stories. This important step, this first contact, has been made.

Before I leave, I still want to take the time to visit Jerusalem, after being invited there by Emma, my interpreter. Like everyone else who arrives in the valley, the white and pink town clinging to the hillsides, the sweeping light of the setting sun, not to mention the weight of 2,000 years of history, offer me a magical combination. Momentarily, I think about becoming a Zionist or a poet, but a tiny detail takes me away from all that beauty: I've had pain in the roof of my mouth and toothache for two days. The famous psalm suddenly comes into my mind: 'If I forget thee, O Jerusalem, let my right hand forget … let my tongue cleave to the roof of my mouth…'

I return to France in more terrible circumstances: some bearded man in a hood, Hamas, Hezbollah or whatever, has blown himself up in front of a cafe in Tel Aviv, 150 metres from where I'd been staying. There are images of pools of blood, debris and shapeless and blackened objects, some of which may be human remains. As is usually the case when such things happen, bearded hysterics on both sides shout, 'Death to the Jews!' or 'Death to the Arabs!' Cowardly, I depart feeling relieved to be going. I'm starting to understand what it means to leave somewhere without being sure that when I return, I'll still find people and things as they were when I left them.

Birkenau, 20 April 1943

This train is rather special. All the arrivals come from a camp near Berlin, a camp built by the German Zionist movement to prepare its militants for the "ascent" in Palestine, the *Aliyah*, by providing them with training in agronomy, agriculture and economics. For a time, until 1941, the Nazis had allowed the camp to operate without much interference, but since then the Gestapo has taken over direct control. Those who remain are no more than detainees, growing vegetables and fruit for the Third Reich, with the camp itself becoming a youth transit camp; a triage to the unknown.

Hilde had been there for a very long time, since her mother was imprisoned. At one point her visa was ready and she had the opportunity to emigrate, but she preferred to stay close to where her mother was. Her experience as a survivor and seniority had given her a certain status among her comrades, who'd got into the habit of consulting her whenever a decision, big or small, needed to be made.

When they arrive on the ramp, they're thrown out of the wagon. It's a welcome they're used to: the Nazis only express themselves by screaming, and ordering them to run when they themselves move rather nonchalantly. The only difference this time for the new arrivals is the attack dogs, and the swarm of inmates dressed in striped rags who take charge of their last possessions after they were left behind in the wagons. Next, they're separated into two columns: men on one side, women on the other. This manic ritual hardly frightens them anymore, having gone through it before already.

Unbeknownst to them, this "selection" is rather unique as they're already considered fit for work, arriving as they have from a youth camp, meaning they'll enter Birkenau as they are. This is how Sylvia, who's 14 and a half years old, but looks about 10, enters the camp with her sister, Carla. They all march in close formation, in a column of five. Sylvia is wearing a long coat she's been given, and the SS hardly notice her as they glance casually down her row.

Their appearance, sheared and shaved, can only be seen in the gaze or comments of others, as there are no mirrors or windows in which they can look at themselves. In Sylvia, tiny and terrified, all you can see are her eyes. Her freshly tattooed arm is painful, and she starts to cry as she sees the chimneys at the back where the smoke billows out into the air. The inmates carrying out the tattooing explain to her, Birkenau style (bluntly), what the chimneys do, and the nature of the place that she finds herself in.

Fifty years later, Sylvia still remembers the vaguely shocked surprise of the manager of Block 9, where she arrives after the second part of the ritual of entering Birkenau, which involves the shearing, shaving, showering, and disinfecting: 'How did we let that one in? She's just a kid!' The *Blockowa*, however, always makes sure that at every rollcall, Sylvia is placed in the back row. We're not allowed to treat her "normally", and she has no place in the camp. Having arrived with scarlet fever, she's protected, staying in the Block and not going to work. It's a semi-clandestine existence. Yet it doesn't protect her against typhus, Flecktyphus, and the whole range of diseases that you catch in quarantine.

Telling her story fifty years later, Sylvia remembers two details about her deportation to Birkenau, two strange peculiarities relating to her transportation. She arrived on 20 April, Hitler's fifty-fourth birthday, and that day Goebbels had given him a present by sending two trains of Jews, the last in Berlin, to hell. One of the trains was bound for Theresienstadt, the other for Birkenau. There were now no longer officially any Jews in Berlin. And even those in hiding numbered only a handful. But her transport had actually left Berlin on the 19th, the day of the Jewish Passover, the commemoration of the exodus from Egypt. An improvised Seder, the feast during which, traditionally, each Jew is a king in his country, was conducted in the cattle wagon. The irony of the situation strikes me.

Chapter 9

Tochter aus Elysium[13]

New York, April 1997

After the experience of my trip to Israel, and the anguish that I had to go through the whole process for nothing, I contact Yvette by phone and then cross the Atlantic. Yvette is the fourth member of the group that no longer remembers you. After the Israelis, I accept this as the norm, merely an objective fact that doesn't merit discussion. My contact so far with her has been quite surprising, and I feel like I've been speaking with a very young girl who's a little intimidated talking to an adult. She has a very clear voice, and a delicious, childish laugh that's crystalline and light. We make a date for the following week, and I worry that by entering her world I'll be like the proverbial bull in a china shop. I have to repeat who I am three times, as well as when I'm arriving, and why it is I want to see her.

I'm staying with some distant family members who, in a stroke of luck, live only a stone's throw away from Yvette in New York. Their political views, especially on Israeli politics, are the polar opposite of mine – we don't discuss it – but they're otherwise very kind and go out of their way to make my stay easier, such as lending me an apartment and driving me around in their car.

In the hallway of Yvette's house, a cosy Long Island pavilion in the affluent New York suburbs, is a copy of some piano sheet music,

---

13. 'Daughter of Elysium' – a reference to Beethoven's hymn *Ode to Joy*, lyrics by Schiller.

Beethoven's *Pathétique*. Yvette certainly isn't what I expected after our phone conversation. Indeed, she's the complete opposite. I'd imagined a nice old woman, fairly sturdy, a little worn out and rather absent minded. In reality, she's tall, slim, lively and active. Her brown hair containing a few silver threads is pulled back in a ponytail, revealing a beautiful face that has been barely marked by time. She's in the middle of preparing lunch for us, a delicious Greek dish, and her husband Jim leaves us alone to talk.

*   *   *

Yvette's memory mainly focusses on two periods; her own journey, and that of her sister Lily, from Thessaloniki to the Birkenau orchestra, and then the circumstances of their liberation, when she must have been saved with an unbelievable amount of luck. Life in the orchestra, the details of everyday life, and even the faces of fellow students, are often very blurry, if not forgotten entirely. The daily horror, the massacres and the routine and mechanical deaths have melted into an oppressive magma in which only a few faces, absurd details, her music lessons, Alma's arrival, and shouting matches with Lili or Sylvia manage to surface.

Strangely, even though our twenty-hour interview takes place in English – Yvette can speak French but is more comfortable in the English that she's been speaking every day for the last fifty years – she still uses the French, in a singing accent, for the names of Little Julie, Big Hélène or Big Fanny. Despite the major trauma she experienced in her youth, this aspect of her language – or languages – has still managed to survive.

Although it seems obvious now, I believe it's thanks to Yvette that I better understand the fact that to survive physically and mentally in Birkenau, a price had to be paid. Yvette tells me that since her imprisonment, she still lacks any kind of self-confidence and is unable, for example, to play the piano in front of anyone other than her husband. She was only able to play the *Pathétique* for Lily on the condition that she went outside and didn't look at her. Technically, however, she was certainly up to the task: she worked with [the American pianist] Murray Perahia, a former student of her sister's, before he started giving concerts in New York. She tells me that she was rather adventurous in her younger years, before the war, but is now afraid of everything: travel, the unknown, and violence in all its forms.

I refuse to try to make a directory, a guide to the effects of Birkenau on you and your former comrades. However, I can't help but wonder: 'Did anyone come out of there unscathed?' Hilde told me: 'When you've been to Auschwitz, you can never leave it completely. When you haven't been there, you can never truly understand...'

Bergen-Belsen, March/April 1945
Lily is dying.

Tripping in the snow, weakened by hunger and cold, she broke her leg and now finds herself completely helpless for the first time in her life. The *Revier* is nothing more than a place where people die, and she'd rather not go. However, she can no longer obtain food and has only her sister to help her. Yvette, meanwhile, is completely disorientated and can only despair and pray, which angers Lily and weakens her even further. The little plump, lively woman is no more than a shadow, but she still has a bad temper.

Their universe has shrunk even further, occupying only the single space they define: one to survive, the other to help it do so. As a result, Helga and Lotte, who were with them initially, disappeared without the sisters realizing it; they either died or were transferred elsewhere. Frau Kroner, who was in their Block when they first arrived, died of typhus a few months after her sister, Maria. She died quietly, just as she had lived. The girls from the orchestra, who'd decided to stay together as much as possible, are now separated and scattered in several Blocks. Some of the Germans – Anita, Hilde, Carla and Sylvia – are with the French and Belgians. Renate, as well.

In Birkenau they'd received food rations which seemed to have been calculated to just below the minimum number of calories needed to survive. Now, since the spring, nothing seems to have been measured like that. There's little or no water, while the food, which is fouler and even less nutritious than before, is distributed randomly. Typhus and dysentery soon set in, wreaking even more terrible havoc than in Birkenau. As the promiscuous nature of the situation increases, the epidemics become all the more devastating. The only scant consolation is that even the Nazis themselves are affected, and some, despite being better fed and cared for, are carried away in a few days.

The sick are piling up at the *Revier* as the nurses scramble as best they can to find medicine, or at least those who don't try to barter with the little stock the Nazis allocate to them. People drop dead like flies. The tiny number of doctors struggle desperately against the onslaught in appalling hygienic conditions, and in the surrounding suffering, your universe is restricted to just yourself and the friends around you. That last circle of humanity at the bottom of the abyss. The bodies of the day's victims pile up in front of the entrance, and no one arrives to pick them up for burial or to burn them.

It's been utter chaos since March, and the Nazis are overwhelmed. The atmosphere is like that of the end of the world. The camp population swells disproportionately as detainees from other camps, further to the east, arrive. Even though it's dying, without knowing what to else to do, the Nazi beast cannot be separated from its slaves. They arrive from all over, in increasingly pitiful states; some having walked for several weeks in convoys harassed by their increasingly hysterical guards, who finish off anyone who collapses from exhaustion along the way by shooting them at the side of the road.

The orchestra women are also exhausted, and exhaust themselves even more in trying to support each other. Anita has dysentery and can no longer retain any liquids, so the other girls come to visit her at the *Revier*. They give her any morsel of food they can find, such as shards of potatoes in their daily soup, so that she can at least eat something more solid and stop wasting away.

* * *

Isn't this where you caught typhus, my poor little mother? Was it the desolation of the place that got the better of your meticulous hygiene and your will to fight, or, more simply, was it the fact that Dora remained behind in Birkenau and you had no more reason to resist? The group of women that supported you, and in which you obviously played your own role with great success, was dislocated. Did this end-of-the-world atmosphere almost undo your final defences?

* * *

In desperation, Lily asks her sister to do her best to find her something solid to eat, and not the translucent soup they're otherwise given. Yvette has an utterly crazy idea and immediately puts it into action. She sets out to confront Irma Griese, who's in the middle of her daily rollcalls. Seeing her staring at her, Griese reacts in the typical SS way to such a situation, giving Yvette a brutal slap and sending her back to her Block. In Belsen, just as it is everywhere else in Hitler's collapsing empire, there's still no excuse for standing there and gawping!

With a buzzing head, Yvette goes to see her sister to tell her what's happened, and the lively Lily immediately sees what to do with the situation: 'Go back and tell her who you are. You were one of her favourites in the orchestra and she'd often stand in front of you when you were playing the accordion. That should do the trick.'

Convinced that this time Griese was actually going to kill her, Yvette nevertheless returns to the same position where the Nazi had struck her only a short while before: her sister's life is certainly worth risking her own. Just before she lets go of her dog, Griese recognizes her: 'You're the Birkenau accordionist! How's your sister, the one who was so fat?'

Yvette tells her about the situation and begs her to put her on a job where she can find something to feed Lily. 'I see,' says Griese, 'Come with me and I'll assign you work in the kitchens. You'll be able to get what you need there.'

As part of her new assignment, every day Yvette now has to carry the 40-litre buckets of soup that make up a Block's rations. The soup itself isn't particularly rich to say the least, and the whole thing is rather heavy. Despite being warm and sheltered, the moist atmosphere in the kitchens makes her even more fragile, and her new task quickly proves to be beyond her strength. Exhausted, at night she tells Lily that she's not going to last much longer.

Being either monstrously selfish, or superbly clairvoyant, Lily orders her sister to go back to Griese and request she be assigned to a less arduous job. Against the odds, and either amused by the young girl's daring, or genuinely eager to help (who knows?), the Nazi returns with Yvette to the kitchens and gives her the job of cleaning the *Kommando*'s Block. As well as cleaning the floor and making the beds, her new role sometimes involves her throwing out the corpses of those who've died during the night.

Yet Yvette finds what she's looking for, what she needs to help Lily survive. But at the same time, she also finds the thing that nearly kills her: a mouldy piece of cheese that's been forgotten about on top of the cutlery cupboard for weeks. It almost fatally poisons her sister, but Lily soon regains her health, and a few days later the British arrive.

In an ironic reversal of roles, a now unconscious and almost delusional Yvette is taken to the hospital by an angry Lily, determined that her sister isn't going to die *after* the liberation. Seized with inspiration, she concocts a dreadful mixture composed of charcoal and powdered coffee donated by the English, and forces Yvette to drink, while at the same time arguing with others that making her drink such a concoction in the first place is going to kill her anyway. 'If she doesn't open her mouth immediately then it's not the drink that's going to kill her, it's me!'

Fifty years later, Yvette still doesn't know if she was saved by divine intervention, her sister's Herculean anger as she forbid her from dying, or her own will to survive at any cost. In reality, she knows it was a mixture of all three.

Paradoxically, it was Yvette's illness that saved her from the fate that killed several thousand prisoners after the departure of the Nazis and the arrival of the liberators: the overabundance of rich food that was impossible to digest for bodies as dilapidated as theirs.

New York, April 1997
Yvette is very proud of her children and grandchildren. I meet Peggy, her daughter, who wanted to know me, and Sean, her grandson. Dark-haired and slender, Peggy looks a lot like her younger mother, judging from the photos I've seen. Yvette is convinced that the little boy, aged 3, will be a great musician as he's shown a good feel for rhythm and music. Her son, David, is currently touring Japan with a symphony orchestra where he plays the viola. Lily's son, meanwhile, is a cellist. A dynasty of musicians. Sean's great-grandmother, the little Jewish woman from Thessaloniki who loved music so much, would no doubt have been very proud of all of them.

Thessaloniki, spring 1943

A new rabbi of Ashkenazi descent, possibly with even a bit of German, has arrived in Thessaloniki's nearly 1,000-year-old Jewish community, and has already divided opinion in the Sephardic society. One of the first things he does after arriving is to hand over the names of each member of the community to the Nazis, who've taken over the occupation of the city from the Italians. Everyone thinks he's a fool for doing so.

Some time later the Thessaloniki Jews, who until this point hadn't had too much to complain about when it came to their occupiers, find themselves locked in a ghetto in the poorest part of town. Next they are gathered together by families and into groups and sent to a transit camp, from where they will then be sent to an unknown destination. They're ordered to take provisions and water with them for a ten-day trip, with the Jews no doubt believing they are being sent to a labour camp somewhere in Germany.

Yvette is in the camp with her father, mother, her sister Lily, and her brother Michel. Also with them are her uncle, aunt and cousins. The whole family is there, the Spanish Jews who'd travelled all around the Mediterranean before settling in Greece. Well-off, Yvette's mother has ambitions for her children, as well as her own personal frustrations: she desperately wanted to be a musician, to master an instrument. Instead, it is her children who will achieve this for her. In charge of the family's radio set, she floods their ears with classical music morning, noon and night. Michel and Lily are learning the piano, and Yvette started to study the basics at the age of 3, usually under duress. Lily makes her work hard and is merciless: any mistake is greeted with a slap on the fingers with a ruler. Much older than her little sister, Lily is authoritarian, severe and often despotic with her younger sibling, so much so that their mother often has to intervene so that Yvette has some time away from her.

The three children are gifted, and their mother encourages them to learn as much as possible: you never know when it might be useful. As Yvette grows up she starts to learn the accordion, before being bought a double bass, which was gigantic in scale. Too small to play it, she'll have to wait before she can start learning how to play: strong fingers are needed to exert the necessary pressure on the strings in order to produce the right sound. As a result, the double bass takes pride of place in a corner of the apartment, like a stage mark, an obligatory rite of passage. Yvette looks at it from time to time, puzzled. Curious and rather whimsically, she agrees to play the double bass if she can also learn to play the drums. If she learns the drums, it'll mean another six months of lessons. But all of this will be left behind when they have to leave for the ghetto.

In April 1943, Michel and Lily are already experienced musicians and for several months have been playing in a club frequented by *Wehrmacht* soldiers. This helps to increase the family income, especially now that resources are very tight after their father's partner was responsible for defrauding the bank. Galloping inflation has also meant the price of basic foodstuffs such as bread and fruit have multiplied several hundred times. Sometimes Yvette goes with her older siblings to the club, where they have to keep a close eye on their young sister. With her dark hair, dark complexion, delicate face and slender waist, she's popular with the male customers, especially the Germans. Michel and Lily make her play a few tunes on the accordion to show off her virtuosity and impress the clients, and occasionally she even replaces the drummer in the orchestra. In return, she's given some money or fruit.

The last happy family event before the cataclysm will be Lily's wedding, to a musician, of course. When the family is summoned by the Gestapo, Michel and Lily are told they don't have to go to the ghetto and must continue to entertain the troops. Yvette chooses to stay with them, thinking she'll be able to see some of the country. Saying goodbye to her parents is a terrible experience:

Yvette still has the vision of her mother as she stood in front of her, in tears, her hands outstretched towards her. The pain is still there. Soon it is their turn to leave, and they travel with their uncle, aunt and cousins for eight days, in incredibly harsh conditions, before arriving in Poland.

* * *

When Yvette and her sister reach Birkenau, they suffer the same selection process as all the other inmates who arrive at the camp. However, Yvette very nearly misses her chance: as she gets off the train, she's all set to go off with her aunt and cousins. After all, an older person would doubtless know how to guide them through this incomprehensible world in which they'd just arrived. But intuitively, Lily grabs her by the hand and forces her to stay by her side. 'Stay with me and shut up!' she scolds.

Next they undergo the obligatory rite of passage when entering the camp; the undressing, shaving, showering and tattooing. The tattoo on her arm hurts, but when she sees Lily with a shaved head, she can't help but find the image rather funny: 'You look like Michel!' She immediately becomes serious again and the fear quickly returns. Where is their brother, where are their parents, their family?

From the moment they enter quarantine, they're asked what they do for a living, among many other inane questions about their origin, their place of birth, and identity. Lily replies straight away: the only thing she really knows how to do is play music. What's more, in Thessaloniki (was that already almost a month ago? It seems like an eternity…) she was able to see how much the Germans also liked music. Lily is definitely a survivor at heart, and she knows that by providing something the Germans want, i.e. music, this could be exchanged for food, favours and simply the right to live.

Under normal circumstances, Yvette would've responded to this ridiculous question with a burst of laughter. How can you ask a 15-year-old child if she has a job? But when asked if she can do anything with her hands, she replies that she also plays the piano and accordion. Initially afraid that the person questioning her will simply laugh in her face, they simply nod their head, write something on their card, and wave her on.

After a few days, she's forgotten where she is. The passing of time takes on a different character here: unbeknownst to her, she's entered into Auschwitz time, where every day looks the same and the minutes tick by like hours. Perhaps it's because they're stolen minutes, lived in a place where only one thing is expected of you; that you die.

In the beginning, when she asks where her uncle, her aunt, and her cousins are, she's given the usual Birkenau answer: she's shown the chimney and is told how that's the only way out of this place. At first, she thinks the people telling her this are crazy. But soon she learns the truth, even discovering later that her two cousins, twin sisters, died together, one having decided that she couldn't bear to survive without the other.

*   *   *

Lily and Yvette hug each other close during the night. It's cold. Polish winters are harsh, and the girls are from the south, where the sun is. Soon after her arrival, Yvette is assigned a task beyond her capabilities. One of the workers has been taken ill and she's been ordered to replace them, meaning she has to carry bricks all day long at one of the camp's exterior sites. By the time it's their "lunch" break in the middle of the day, she's already too exhausted to eat, and when she returns to the Block in the evening, she confides in her sister that she'll be dead soon.

Then the unimaginable happens. A *Laüferin* enters precisely at this moment and calls out two numbers, hers and Lily's. Their initial reaction is perfectly natural: fear. 'What have we done wrong?' In this place, survival seems to depend upon the specific ability of being able to blend in with the mass of other inmates. To be singled out often results in being beaten, usually with a stick, in an act of extra misery that further undermines any resistance.

They're led out to Camp B, and arrive at a Block that's still under construction. Stunned, they see four women sitting there motionless, with guitars on their knees. On a table in front of them are music scores and even a few sheets, transcribed by Michel, whose writing they quickly recognize. They can hardly hide their relief at knowing he's still alive.

A young woman with a round face and large brown eyes looks at them. Her name is Mala Zimetbaum. Struck by Yvette's youth, she gives her a jumper and some bread, her privileged position meaning she can easily obtain similar favours. 'You're musicians, accordionists? Play something and show us what you can do.' Zofia Tchaïkowska, Blockowa and senior conductor, introduces herself. She takes a score at random and hands it over. The sisters realize that this is an audition. Lily has played the piece before, mostly very well, but on piano, not the accordion. She pretends to play with both hands, while only playing the notes on the right-hand side of the instrument, the one designed like a small piano keyboard. 'Don't worry', whispers Yvette, 'I'll help you out with the base notes.'

Tchaïkowska is such a poor musician that she doesn't even realize what's going on; that there are only three hands playing the instruments and not four. Nevertheless, she seems satisfied (maybe she doesn't have any other options?), and Yvette and Lily are officially made members of the orchestra.

* * *

From now on the accordions, which are far more powerful and sonorous instruments than the flutes, lead the way at the head of the orchestra as it makes its way to the gates. Yvette is at the front, in the first row on the left, and is the one who sets the pace for the rest of the group to follow. Lily is next to her, and her technique improves quickly; she's a talented musician.

Marching in their rows of five, once the distance between the Block and the gate (about 800 metres) has been covered, they arrange themselves in the order designated to them in the music room and begin to string together military marches until the last *Kommando* has passed, before finally returning to the Block, still in step.

Under Tchaïkowska, the music they play isn't particularly demanding. They learn a selection of new marches and try their hand at orchestrations of Polish folk songs. The musicians themselves aren't of a particularly high standard and Tchaïkowska doesn't know how to go about improving them; as a primary school teacher, she previously had only taught music to children. Face with these young women who've been thrown into hell, she doesn't even know how to speak to them, or in what language. Consequently, she either descends into a mad rage or goes and sulks in the study which serves as her bedroom, between the dormitory-dining room and the music room.

Arriving in Birkenau in 1942, Tchaïkowska is one of the few detainees to have survived the early days of the camp, when the whole site was a swamp and there were hardly any sanitation facilities. Living conditions at the time were even more appalling then they are now, especially for women. Although she's tall and strong, this past year has left an indelible mark on her. She's completely unstable, passing through periods of explosive irritability and then depression without warning, and without seemingly being able to escape.

Despite the inconsistencies in her behaviour, the orchestra continues under her direction. Her position as a *Prominent* in the camp puts her in contact with other inmates in the same situation and with a similar status, such as those in charge of the food and clothing depots, meaning she's able to obtain certain favours for her orchestra. Benefits include extra bread, or better-fitting clothes and shoes (shoes that are too small or too big can cause great suffering, if not death, among the regular deportees). In addition, unlike what happens in some other Blocks, she doesn't take a cut from each ration of bread that passes through her hands. She also ensures that the *Stubendienst* distributes the soup evenly by making them stir the mixture – very important! – so that each of the girls gets her share of the few scraps of meat and potatoes which would otherwise remain at the bottom of the bucket – a privilege that's normally reserved for the *Kapos* and their favourites.

She takes the youngest members, Sylvia and Yvette, under her wing as much as she can, calling out 'Yvetka!' every now and then and giving her an extra apple or piece of bread. Yvette is still young and a little bit too naive. During breaks between rehearsals, she leaves the Block and sits outside on the sparse grass; she's increasingly joined by a young woman who seems to be sympathetic and caring, until one day Yvette receives a fiery letter from her which she doesn't understand. She goes to see Tchaïkowska who reads the letter and bursts out laughing, recommending to a stunned Yvetka that she shouldn't go and sit on the grass for a while.

Tchaïkowska also has her favourites, such as Danka Kollakowa, a friend of hers who arrived in Birkenau at the same time, and who had previously been assigned a safe role in *Kanada*. Wanting to be closer to her friend, Tchaïkowska allocates her the cymbals, previously played by a young 14-year-old Greek girl called Liliane, the daughter of Dr Menasche, who plays the flute in the men's orchestra.

Once dismissed from the orchestra, little Liliane doesn't survive. Telling the story to me fifty years later, Yvette is still outraged. Just so she could feel better, Tchaïkowska had allowed her friend, who already occupied a privileged position in *Kanada*, to take the place of a child who otherwise only had the orchestra for protection.

*   *   *

Everything changes when Alma arrives at the end of August. From the outset she places much higher demands on the group and the pace of work intensifies enormously. When she doesn't get what she expects from her musicians, she unleashes a fierce tirade at them. The words she uses can be extremely hurtful, and that's when she's not throwing her conductor's baton in their faces – a tradition first practised by the conductor Arturo Toscanini, which resulted in his musicians at the MET in New York staging a sit-down strike. Lily, a professional musician, doesn't accept being treated in this way and is soon on the verge of revolt, with only an energetic intervention from Yvette and Big Julie preventing her from exploding. Nevertheless, she's punished when she refuses to heed Alma's remarks during her playing, the worst punishment for her seeming to be forced to shut up and submit.

As well as Alma, a further source of concern is Flora, newly arrived from Holland, who also plays the accordion. Three accordionists run the risk of the orchestra being overcrowded, and so Yvette no longer plays during concerts, keeping her role solely for the morning and evening marches. She fears being excluded from the orchestra and having to return to toiling on the roads in a working *Kommando*. After all, Alma has already made some changes that have resulted in the clumsiest or less motivated musicians being removed from the group.

Although she's really starting to push the girls hard, Alma often complains about the lack of substance, of bass, in the orchestra. Suddenly, Lily remembers the double bass intended for Yvette that stood in the corner of their house, and has an idea. She approaches Alma with an astonishing suggestion: why not let Yvette have double bass lessons from the bassist in the men's orchestra? This would solve both the problem of too many accordions, and also add to the overall sound of the ensemble.

Intrigued by the idea, Alma suggests it to Hössler during one of his visits to the Block. Also keen, Hössler asks Yvette how old she is.

'I am 15 and a half. My mother bought me a double bass, but I didn't have time to learn how to play it before I was arrested.'

'And where's your mother?'

Yvette points towards the smoking chimney behind the Block.

'...*Schade* [pity].'

Pity... Has he just realized that the mother of an apprentice bassist – even a Jew – could have something in common with a human being? Wasting no time, Hössler organizes the lessons with the conductor of the men's orchestra and three times a week, the bassist comes to teach Yvette. A break from the daily lethal routine, it also establishes a rare bond between the two camps and will have consequences in the future.

Michel, Lily and Yvette's brother, regularly receives news and messages from his sisters. One day, he accompanies the bassist to the women's camp – a crime that'll be cruelly punished if he's caught. Another musician, Little Julie's brother, a violinist in the men's orchestra and an architect in civilian life, had been discovered trying to send a note to his sister. As punishment, Julie received twenty-five lashes with the whip, while her brother was nearly beaten to death by the guards, who were arguably less sensitive than their leaders to the benefits that music could bring to their daily task of murdering human beings.

Aware of the risk he's taking, Michel equips himself with scores and various instruments before setting off with the bassist. He clears the gate of the men's camp and the road to the gas chambers – the main artery of the entire Birkenau complex – before finally passing through the gate of Camp B and along *Lagerstrasse*.

Entering the orchestra's Block, he sees one of the most powerful SS officers approaching, the *Oberaufsehrin* Maria Mandl, and so turns around runs off at full speed. Mandl gives chase and after catching him up, orders him to explain himself. Michel eventually confesses that he came to see his sisters, the accordionists. As luck would have it, Mandl has a bit of a soft spot for Yvette, and allows him to visit the girls. The incident is over.

Yvette quickly becomes indispensable. The Nazis watch to see what progress she can make, and after a few months are satisfied that she's beginning to improve. Hössler regularly comes to see what's she's doing and, ever the technocrat, stands in front of her and takes notes. Yvette hardly dares to look at him, convinced that it's actually a demon prowling around her.

And so this is how, in the shadow of the gas chambers and in the foul smoke of the crematoria, people were also able to give and receive music lessons in Birkenau.

Chapter 10

Polonaises

Warsaw – Krakow, spring 1997

Rarely have I hated a city so much. Warsaw stinks. It's ugly, having been rebuilt after the war in that Stalin-style from the 1950s that did so much to promote the glory of socialism in Eastern Europe: straight, over-wide avenues designed to serve as additional landing strips for bombers in the event of a transition from the "cold" war to a "hot" war with the West; sad and degraded concrete blocks, and, of course, a carbon copy of the Moscow University building, although here it was called the Palace of Culture and Science. Opposite the hideous central station, the "palace" is framed by a Holiday Inn and a rowdy Marriott Hotel. The people here are poor, and as soon as I leave the airport I get swindled by a taxi driver. I'm harassed every two minutes for what I suppose is money: for the first time in my life, I can't understand a word of the language I'm hearing.

I feel oppressed and overwhelmed by the place the moment I get off the plane. I'm not naïve enough to believe that it's just the ugliness causing me to feel this way. The sound of Poland also affects me painfully, even to the point of anguish. After a night in a city-centre hotel, I take a train to escape and suddenly something takes hold of me: a suffocating feeling, with cold sweats and heart pains. I'm travelling to Krakow to meet Helena, but I'm also travelling towards Birkenau.

The depression and anguish I was struggling with flies away as soon as I arrive in Krakow, and I fall in love with the city from the first sightseeing tour I make with Marcin, my Polish interpreter. He tells me several anecdotes about the city, including some about the houses built in various styles over the centuries: Italian, medieval Slavic, Renaissance, Baroque... It's a cacophony of colours and architectural styles which, instead of clashing, create an extraordinary harmony. He takes me to what is probably the most beautiful bookshop in the world, set up in a gigantic colonnaded room. I breathe more freely. The people here seem to be nicer, younger, possibly more beautiful, and I begin to feel at home.

Marcin isn't entirely a neutral when it comes to my project. His father, a political deportee, was detained at Auschwitz in 1940, but miraculously survived his ordeal; his mother was deported to Ravensbrück. A whole lifetime of silences and secrets kept hidden "for the children's sake", just like me.

I had to press Helena quite hard for her to agree to meet me. After an initially positive response, two days before my departure from Paris she asked me not to come because Zofia had quite a serious illness, and I think she only changed her mind reluctantly. After all, you can't force people to stir up memories like these.

Helena welcomes us to her home one afternoon, and I instantly have an affection for her. She's very small, with clear eyes and the serious face of a teenager who had to grow up too quickly. In this small, concrete block apartment on the outskirts of Krakow, you could imagine yourself in a quiet pre-war Polish interior. There's nothing flashy about the place, but everything is clean and meticulously tidy. I see musical instruments, a desk, books, photographs, icons. She often takes her time before speaking, seemingly weighing up what I'm saying against what she knows to be true herself before responding. When something comes to mind, she often says 'Aha!' and nods her head vigorously. After a while, charmed, I look forward to this interjection.

Birkenau, November 1943

Helena and her mother have been under the hands of the Nazis for several months, having unwittingly housed Resistance cadres. Since their arrest – after being denounced – in January 1943, they've already served several months in prison in Lwów (Lviv), their hometown, in extremely difficult conditions. Naively believing that things couldn't get any worse, Helena and her mother now find themselves in quarantine, in Block 25 which, for the moment, isn't serving as an anteroom to the gas chamber.

As a violinist who'd graduated from a conservatory, Helena announces that she's a musician as soon as she arrives in Birkenau. She passes the audition without any objection from Alma, and quickly finds herself as a member of the orchestra. Having learned about the function of Block 25, however, she worries about her mother's fate. She knows what conditions the quarantine inmates have to suffer, being constantly threatened with typhus and dysentery, and fears that her mother, aged 55, won't survive. As a result, Helena makes frequent visits to Camp A, and hopes to be able to have her mother assigned to a relatively lenient *Kommando*.

Too shy and still too disoriented to intercede with Mandl on her mother's behalf, Helena can only do one thing when the inevitable happens as her mother contracts dysentery, six weeks after Helena joined the orchestra. She does everything she can to ensure her mother is admitted to the *Revier*, but when it comes to dysentery, where the patient weakens by becoming dehydrated, it's particularly difficult: you have to have a fever in order to be admitted to the *Revier*. With the help of her Polish comrades, however, Helena manages to succeed. She takes her some soup, fruit, toast, and is able to negotiate some glucose shots, again with the help of her friends. Nevertheless, her mother dies soon afterwards, on 2 December 1943.

Krakow, May 1997

Dear Helena,

After a few minor issues, you agreed to meet me, and to entrust me with part of your history in this orchestra. I can only guess how much it cost you to talk about this with someone who hadn't shared your experiences. If one is to strive, as I do, to think about the indescribable, one must at least give up trying to understand it. There are times when what is logical, chronological and coherent has no place, and this is never truer than when one speaks of Birkenau.

Did I force you to talk? Was it too much? To try and think the unthinkable, to name the unspeakable and describe the indescribable? I struggled, and I will undoubtedly continue to struggle for a long time, with this impossibility. I know I have to tell people what I've learned, and I want to do this, but how do you repeat something that's impossible to say, but at the same time has to be said?

You made a cup of tea for Marcin and me, and I saw you bustling about, a good housewife with a very straight silhouette, and direct, precise mannerisms. At home, between the piano and the violin stand, surrounded by your family photographs, the extreme strangeness of my own presence struck me. While I felt morally at ease from contacting you like I did – a story like yours and that of your fellow orchestra comrades can't remain unknown or be lost – I vowed not to make you or any of the other survivors scratch away at your memory until it bleeds, especially if, and when, it had previously almost healed.

You've all had to relearn how to exist in an almost normal world over the "after" [Birkenau] years, and it took a tremendous amount of willpower to do so. In order not to go mad, you have, I think, been forced to block the most dreadful memories from your mind and not carry the burden of Birkenau with you as you try to live your lives. Despite this gruelling task, sometimes raw emotion still reappears, and it did between us.

With great restraint, you spoke to me about the pain caused by the death of your mother. Yet there came a point in your recollection when I felt it necessary to change the subject, when your voice broke, and you were silent for a few seconds. You'd forgotten, "back then", that your mother knew music, and could both read and write it well; it hadn't occurred to you to introduce her as a copyist in the orchestra. You've always blamed yourself for this oversight, as well as blaming yourself for not doing what Anita did for her sister, Renate: speak to Oberaufseherin *Mandl so that she could be assigned a job as a* Läuferin.

After your liberation following the "death march", you regularly go to Birkenau, as we go to visit the cemetery, to pay homage to this mother who you miss and for whom you feel responsible. Your victory over Nazism, yours and that of your surviving comrades, cost you dearly, and you continue to pay for it, still. Two days after your mother's death, you were admitted to the Revier *with typhus, and, whether you meant to or not, you made the connection between the two events in the story you told me. I allowed myself – and allow myself once again – to remind you of what you know deep down. It wasn't your forgetfulness, or your shyness, that killed your mother; it was the Nazis.*

With love,
Jean-Jacques

Birkenau, January 1944

Aided by her friends, Helena leaves the *Revier* a month later. She's already tried to leave earlier, aware that the *Revier* is more like a house of death than a hospital, but barely able to stand, she fainted on her attempt. Kept there until she was "fit" to be released, Helena is visited by her friends, who also bring her food almost every day after the evening roll call.

Alongside these displays of friendship and solidarity between inmates, cracks begin to show among an orchestra that isn't just made up of saints, but of human creatures as well. Although it represents a protected, albeit precarious, enclave in the death camp, the orchestra isn't immune to the inhuman pressure exerted by Birkenau.

Beyond the language barrier, often impassable in this Tower of Babel, an invisible but very powerful line of demarcation divides the company into two distinct and sometimes antagonistic groups: the Jews, who constitute the majority of the workforce, and the Poles, strong, slightly better fed, but also nourished by the most incredible, extreme anti-Semitic superstitions. Some have been in the camp for a longer period of time, having been deported as hostages, or as members of resistance families, and, much more rarely, because they hid Jews. None of the musicians is in the latter case. Still, there are, among them, communists, and women with liberal ideas, but this doesn't prevent anti-Semitism from resurfacing.

The Poles have a somewhat separate status in the camp. Considered to be "Aryan" – which is a shame, given that that they're part of a people the Nazis call "Slavic", and whom they want to employ as slaves of their thousand-year-old Reich – they still have the advantage of not being subjected to "selections". They were also among some of the first to arrive at Auschwitz-1, then Birkenau.

The oldest, Zofia Tchaïkowska, the *Blockowa*, and Sztefania, known as Pane (Madame) Founia, carry the numbers 6873 and 6874, which, in the hierarchy of the camp, marks them out as *Prominenten*: members of the "aristocracy", allowing them to have certain advantages and meaning they can avoid any hard labour. They are responsible for the Blocks, *Kapos*, or work in the camp's administration. Having a four-number "badge" says a lot about their resilience and their ability to navigate and organize themselves in order to survive in this Auschwitz universe. The bonds forged with other older women in the camp give them some additional material privileges which, in turn, ultimately benefit the orchestra as a whole.

In the orchestra, the Polish group makes up around a third of the total number of members. It's a close-knit group, but one of the main elements that unites them is the centuries-old anti-Semitism peculiar to Poland, less "scientific" than that of the Nazis, perhaps, but just as virulent.

*　*　*

They have a separate corner in the dormitory, with their own table which they share with the Russians and Ukrainians, and keep together when they're not playing music. They hardly show any signs of friendship or mix with their other comrades. As the months progress, they all manage to obtain comfortable clothes, stored in a dresser in the music room.

One day, Maria, one of the *Stubendienst*, decides to clear out the chest of drawers and orders that the surplus jumpers be taken back to the *Bekleidungskammer*, the clothing storehouse. Upon learning this, Violette randomly selects one of the jumpers and gives it to a friend who works in the kitchen. A few days later, wearing the jumper in question, the friend comes to see Violette to give her some potatoes. Maria notices jumper and suspects that some black market dealings have taken place. It's a serious accusation and can have dangerous consequences, including being sent to a disciplinary *Kommando*, or even worse. Despite this, she doesn't hesitate for a single second and drags Violette out, ready to take her to the Nazis.

Hélène quickly intervenes, declaring that she'd given the jumper to Violette. Anita also claims she gave her the jumper, as does Fania, followed by a good majority of the Jewish inmates so that in the end, Maria finally gives up her stubborn determination to have

Violette punished. During the course of the argument, not one of the Poles intervened.

Violette and Hélène still bitterly recall similar sordid episodes, which were often related to food. Some of the Polish inmates receive food parcels from families on a fairly regular basis, sometimes even fresh produce such as eggs, butter and fruit. Not being allowed to benefit from such privileges, Jewish prisoners occasionally attend meals where the Poles don't even want to touch their rations. For those whose families send parcels every day, some even empty their plates onto the ground or in the bucket of dirty water, rather than give anything away. At other times they fry eggs or cold meats in makeshift pans, without the slightest concern for others: the smell of melting fat inflicting a genuine torment for those on the edge of starvation. Hélène would later tell me about Fanny's ever-renewed anger, and how you, Elsa, would try to calm her down. As Fanny would say, 'They could at least be more discreet!'

Noticeably less hostile to her Jewish comrades, on one occasion Helena finds herself at the centre of a conflict which, for once, has music at its heart. Blessed with a remarkable memory and a good ability to orchestrate musical parts, Fania has been helping Alma for a while when it comes to expanding the orchestra's repertoire with new pieces of music. One day they decide to take on Beethoven's *Sonata Pathétique* and Fania arranges it for a string quartet. They want to play this kind of music for themselves, for their own entertainment and pleasure, because they love music, and because performing military marches all of the time can only bring limited artistic satisfaction.

The planned line up consists of Little Hélène, Big Hélène, Anita, and Helena, who's been offered the role of second violin. The rehearsals progress well until the moment when, overnight, Helena is suddenly forced to stop playing. In fact, all of the Polish members of the orchestra have given her an ultimatum: either she stops all work and personal contact with the Jews, or she'll be exiled by her compatriots. Any quarantine, isolation, or exclusion from the group is practically a death sentence, and Helena therefore has no choice but to give in, which, in retrospect, no one holds against her. It's sad, both for this stupid manifestation of anti-Semitism, and the missed opportunity, and she tells me how much it cost her, and how it even made her cry.

On 14 July 1944, when the French and Belgians meet in the music room to sing *La Marseillaise*, one of the Poles walks through the door and asks what's going on. As far as she's concerned, for Jewish women to sing any national anthem is absurd at best, and heretical at worst.

Exasperated, Violette and Little Hélène decide one day to organize a punitive expedition. The object is both derisory and symbolic, but the satisfaction obtained is immense. One of the best-nourished Poles has a box full of crumbs and bits of dry cake in her locker, the leftovers of meals and food parcels sent from the outside. The two accomplices seize the box and empty it greedily, savouring every crumb for its calorific value and, in an act of long overdue revenge, share it with whoever wants any. In the end, the owner of the box never dares to complain.

Auschwitz, May 1997

It's a lovely spring day when Marcin, my Polish interpreter, and I first visit the town of Oświęcim, where camp No. 1 was located. I spend the entire drive there in a state of extreme tension, a lump of panic in the pit of my stomach. Childishly, I wonder how Marcin would react if I start crying like a baby when we get there.

After parking in the carpark next to the tour coaches, what strikes me initially is how small the place is, particularly when compared with the representation I have of it in my head. The blocks of buildings made from dirty red bricks, a few wooden casemates and, of course, concrete installations with a mysterious use: a sort of mound on which grass has been sown, surmounted by a chimney in the shape of a parallelepiped, high and rather big. It's a crematorium. Directly ahead is the square where Höss, the first Auschwitz commander, was hanged in 1947.

Auschwitz-1 is now a museum, comprising all that is necessary and unbearable. The rooms in one Block contain a variety of "exhibits": piles of prostheses, glasses, children's clothes and shoes, suitcases with painted white names still visible on their lids, like that of "M. Frank", which could just as well – why not? – have been Margot, Anne Frank's sister. In one of the rooms, a display case shows a relic which tugs at both of our heartstrings: a baby's vest knitted with large stitches, a little muted now, in faded blue and pink colours. Marcin imagines his own son wearing the vest, while I, who never had children of my own, imagine the babies I used to look after, in my life "before"…

Other Blocks describe the living conditions of French, Czech and Polish detainees, and there's a photograph of Alma Rosé in the Block dedicated to the Austrian prisoners. At the museum entrance is a very heavily moralistic exposition of the Nazi aggression against Poland, the occupation, the resistance and, finally, the liberation. It all sounds like an official speech from the Stalinist era; the occupation is naturally "ferocious", the resistance "heroic", with the "Soviet big brother" saving the day after the "sacrifice of 40 million dead…" A few signs, however, have clearly been replaced more recently, such as those which previously spoke of the prominent role of the Red Army.

Next to the entrance, in one of the Blocks, is a bookshop flanked by a cafeteria where drinks, sandwiches and burgers are served. Where's the McDonald's? A film montage, produced by the Soviet Army when the camp was liberated in January 1945, is shown in the projection room next to the cafeteria.

You can go on a guided tour or follow your own route, with technical but relevant commentary on how people were gassed and incinerated in the gas chamber and crematoria at the back of the camp. The guide points out the rails that run between the gas chamber and the ovens, and coolly describes the actions of the inmates charged with this task. There's no anger, no revolt, no disgust, he just does his job as a guide, efficiently. Bumping into the tour again in the basement of Block No. 11, the "Block of death", the guide yells at us because we aren't respecting the purpose of the visit and are disrupting the route of the people under his wing. A group of young Israelis are on the guided tour. They're all dressed in blue and white, the colours of the national flag that many have brought along with them, and most of them are wearing a jacket marked "EL AL".

Parents are there with their children, some of them very small. A father caries his child's dummy as the toddler stares wide-eyed at the displays in the Block of "exhibits". In solidarity with the child, I ask Marcin: 'What the hell are they doing here, these children?' And I ask myself the same question. Marcin tells me that, under Gomulka,[14*] Auschwitz visits were obligatory for school children, and how he himself suffered three sleepless nights after his first visit, aged 11.

Everything becomes increasingly irrelevant to me, and whilst having a coffee in the cafeteria, I decide to go straight to Birkenau, 3 kilometres away.

I've requested a search be made for your name in the archives, as well as one for my grandfather, for Lydia and for her parents, Rosa and David. I'm under no illusions, however: Rosa and Lydia were surely gassed as soon as they arrived — a little girl and her mother were the essence of what Nazism was destroying. They probably weren't even registered as part of the camp workforce. As for David, you, and my grandfather, I had nothing more than a one

---

14. Władysław Gomułka was a Polish communist politician. He was the de facto leader of post-war Poland from 1947 until 1948. Following the Polish October, he became leader again from 1956 to 1970.

Lydia (front, centre) with her parents (second and third from right) in Belgium.

in twenty chance of finding something. This is because on leaving the camp during the chaos of January 1945, the SS nevertheless took the time to blow up the crematoria in Birkenau; they'd already burned 95 per cent of the archives there on 31 October 1944, the day after your transfer to Belsen.

The overload of stupid explanations and images to which we're subjected becomes oppressive. I find the noise unbearable: the figures of the living scattered like tourists throughout the site cover the shadows of fifty years ago so much so that I can hardly see them anymore. As I leave, I notice buildings on the other side of the road in the same style and colour, behind cedar hedges: the houses and barracks of the SS who guarded the camp. They're still lived in today, and at the corner of the road is the famous shop whose opening created such a strong reaction. It's not even a supermarket, just a simple corner shop in a small provincial town.

This sinister alignment of buildings on either side of the road, uniform in their ugliness, is far more evocative to me than the heavy pedagogy implemented in the museum. Only a larger photograph spoke to me, and for good reason. To the right of the wrought-iron gate, adorned with the famous *Arbeit macht frei*, is a small building in a small square. It must have been a guard post, and on its wall is an enlarged portion of a photograph taken by a member of the SS in 1940 or 1941. It shows the men's camp orchestra, playing at the same location. There are about ten of them, dressed almost normally, and seated on what appear to be garden chairs. Meanwhile, the conductor is perched on kind of white wooden box. There are a few violinists, flutes, and an accordion. In front of them, on the open ground, the massed inmates are stood listening.

Brzezin, 2 May 1997

This was the first time that I'd physically been in the place where, in a way that was always so incomprehensible to me, I think you've always remained. Where you've returned to, but from where I believe you were never completely released. My presence here, on this incredible but vital journey that I've undertaken, was always inevitable.

What can one say about Birkenau? Who can you confide in when you return to it so often in your nightmares? How do I tell people that I'd hardly dare walk in certain areas, right down at the far end, behind what remains of the gas chambers and crematoria, in what are now glades and undergrowth? Fifty years have passed, the birches have grown, the grass has covered the ashes and the mass graves, but when you last saw them, these places had a whole other function than that of an open-air museum.

The wind blows over the whole site; 300 barracks, 160 hectares, figures of people, but also, above all, the indescribable. The billions of seconds that have passed one by one, suffered by all those individuals who were martyred there.

I have to search for the topographical landmarks, 'this is where they went to play music, this must be where their Block was, this is the path that the man who gave double bass lessons to Yvette had to take,' all the time trying not to become lost in a whirlwind of images rehashed a thousand times in my head. Using a map Violette had drawn for me, I'm able to locate the main places linked to you. Helena had also shown me the routes you would have taken, this time on a more official map, one of those that abound in the museum's many bookshops.

Surprised and then terrified not to hear, as the saying goes, "your fifty-year-old cry", I explain to Marcin, in a manner as pedantic as one of the tour guides, the function of such-and-such a building. I start praying in order to cover the silence. However, I believe you can discover Birkenau in any which way you chose: it doesn't learn anything, it doesn't speak, it only echoes back. Suffering isn't material, yours nor any other. It's not swept away from the floors of the barracks, nor is it inscribed in the stones that still stand, or in the walls that are being laboriously restored, as *Kanada* is currently being, laying under a plastic sheet whilst the work is carried out. The wind that seems to constantly sweep through the place only raises a yellowish dust, it doesn't carry the stench of insane misery that you thought perhaps you'd never be rid of.

The only echo returned here is just that of my own thoughts, my own visions, and of the words that your comrades had entrusted to me. It's in my memory that your presence is the strongest. The maps I've studied before, the photographs I've looked at, the various books I've read, are nothing; this amplified echo I sense here is what matters. And so, imbued with the place as I am, I know no more than before, and I admit that I'm still only able to understand a tiny part of what was done to you.

How difficult it is then to have pity, respect, and regret for all those who've passed through here in their hundreds of thousands, those who have returned and those who didn't! You can only let your hand drag, as I did, over a rotting koya, or over a drawing of a church tower on a wall that's been almost erased. You can only fleetingly caress the bricks of a stove around which you would've toasted bread, where you warmed yourself and chatted with your fellow prisoners when the cold weather struck. Yes, I am in your Block, or what remains of it. Just a rectangle of bricks marking the periphery and the foundations for the wooden walls, the debris of two stoves, all of it invaded by grass dotted with dandelions and anemones. It's a surprise and a shock; after all, it's no uglier or a different colour than any other grass in the world.

But what you went through there can't really be felt. I walk for five hours across the whole site, Camp A, Camp B, the Gypsy camp, the families' camp, the men's camp, the ruins and twisted scrap metal of the crematoria, the ash-spreading fields, and yet this period of your life is still inaccessible to me. I'm not so naive as to believe that it is locked in the stones of *Lagerstrasse* or the somewhat rickety bricks, as the genie in Aladdin's lamp might have been, only waiting for my arrival to show itself. My coming here hasn't changed the mystery. Birkenau is still unimaginable to me, and the disaster you experienced here still incomprehensible.

Why is it that my eyes blur as I write this, and why do I no longer feel like the same person anymore since going "there"?

Krakow, May 1997
After two visits to Helena – as well as the trip to Auschwitz that I was so apprehensive about – I learn that Zofia has agreed to meet me, perhaps reassured by what her friend has told her about me.

One of the first things she tells me, in a slightly wry tone, is how she's always been discouraged from talking about the subject with people who haven't been there. She immediately recognises you in me when she sees me smile and, after the Birkenau ordeal, it's a rather heart-warming feeling.

Zofia is also very small, and appears to be rather weak and sick. Her deep voice, however, is firm and composed, and it's clearly her who's conducting the interview rather than the other way around. Surprised, I let her continue. Of all the ones I've met, Zofia is the only one who prepared for our interview by writing notes. On several occasions she reads me excerpts from articles written for various journals, including one for the Auschwitz Museum. On your behalf, she reads me extraordinary passages full of warmth and esteem, and at various points that seemed important to your story, she punctuates her speech with her hand, as Helena nods along in agreement.

There's obviously the same indissoluble bond between these two women as there was between you, Hélène and Fanny. Zofia agrees with this; when she encountered problems after returning home, it was with her friends from the camp rather than with her own family that she sought solution, help or comfort. She talks about the weight she's carried with her over all of these years, but also tells me how she finally managed to leave her ordeals behind her. After the liberation, she was unable to listen to music for over ten years. She would force herself to attend concerts, only to return home physically ill. But time eventually healed the wound. A great deal of time.

Helena, more able-bodied, makes some tea, and, using the affectionate diminutive Helenka, Zofia asks her if she can bring some sugar or more water. There doesn't appear to be a relationship of dependency or authority between them. Although the sick Zofia is physically dependent on Helena, everything seems to be very normal. As the interview progresses, Zofia grows more cheerful and slightly less formal. In the beginning, she answers my questions with a solemn *Pana* (Mr), then a pause. By the end, she feels able to call me "Jan", Jean-Jacques perhaps being too hard for her to pronounce. Or perhaps it's another charming diminutive that she's composed on the spot.

Birkenau, May 1943

A political deportee and newly arrived in Auschwitz, Zofia is unable to come to terms with what's happened. She refuses to join the orchestra, despite the announcement made by a *Läuferin*, then by Marylka, one of the musicians, in the Quarantine Block. However, one of her Block comrades points her out, almost denouncing her, as a violinist; she'll play whether she likes it or not. Told of her existence and her reluctance to join, Tchaïkowska summons Zofia before her and, as a welcome, proceeds to give her a hard slap. 'This is for not volunteering for something when any normal person would give their right eye to be here! Now I want you to play so that I can see if you're any good.' She hands her a score, which Zofia proceeds to massacre. Morally, she clearly doesn't feel capable of playing it. But Tchaïkowska isn't fooled. Perhaps you have to be a really good musician, or at least more technically efficient than Zofia is, to play wrong the wrong notes intentionally.

She receives another slap for her unwillingness and is practically forced to join. As if for her own benefit, whilst slapping her Tchaïkowska also hits her with some basic home truths. She's trying to do all she can for the girls, especially the young ones, to integrate them into the orchestra so as to give them an extra chance of survival. Trying not to sabotage her hard-fought efforts should be the least one could do!

Shortly afterwards, Zofia dares to approach Hössler to request a transfer to a "normal" *Kommando*, one without special privileges, and without being obliged to play for the Nazis every morning. What's more, one without having to endure the sight of her fellow inmates, exhausted and sick, parading past each morning and evening as part of a killing machine that vampirizes their last ounce of life, before repossessing them as nothing more than industrial waste.

Unlike other members of the orchestra, Zofia is unable to take refuge in the imaginary world of music, and doesn't feel tormented by an irresistible desire to live. She remains permanently conscious of the demented hell in which she's found herself, and despite the privileges of her new role as a violinist in the orchestra, her torture continues unabated. She's told by the SS that the only possible alternative is a transfer to a disciplinary *Kommando*, with her death guaranteed within three weeks. Despite her prejudices, and at the cost of permanent depression, Zofia enters the orchestra. Fifty years later, she still hasn't really forgiven herself. She sits with the violins, alongside two other Poles, Wisha and Irena, the oldest women in the group apart from Frau Kroner, and, from September onwards, with Violette. The arrival of Little Hélène and Little Julie allows Alma, who succeeded Tchaïkowska, to establish a fourth violin section, and Zofia is added alongside the two French speakers.

Despite her depressed state, Zofia quickly bonds with Wisha and Marylka, who arrived almost at the same time as her, then later with Helena, who arrives in early November. Once the trauma of landing on planet Birkenau has passed, the four of them form a kind of family nucleus that helps support each other, as well as the other members of the orchestra as a whole. One can survive – for a while – by being united in this demoralizing place, where mothers eat their own children's bread ration, and where you can steal the basic means of survival, a mess tin, a spoon, or a pair of shoes.

Chapter 11

The Dying Swan

Netzer Sereni, May 1997

As I visit each of the women, I put them all in contact with one another, updating them as I go, which for some reason or other pleases me. It's a bit like reviving a dormant network, knowing that some of them haven't seen or spoken each other for more than fifty years. As a result, I was responsible for giving Hilde a recording of a film about Anita, produced by the BBC.

Now I understand why I'm happy to be the messenger; it wasn't just about paying my share in exchange for them helping me with my project. Above all, it is a way of inserting myself into this ancient group, now spread all over the world, and of being a part of it while at the same time allowing myself to be useful. Thanks to Zofia, Helena and Violette, I now know more about Hilde, things she didn't want to tell me herself.

She had a special place in this group of "half-silly" girls, as Sylvia would call them. Honest and attentive to others to the point of obsession, she acted as a guarantee or even a moral conscience. She watched over the youngest girls, Yvette and Sylvia, supporting and encouraging them with a caress, a kind word, or more if necessary. Sylvia remembers how she was literally starving when she returned from the *Revier* after having typhus, and Hilde simply handed over her food ration to help her recover. Like you, she tried to mitigate any misunderstandings resulting from language barriers, but also managed to gain the respect of everyone, including the Poles, or at least those who weren't particularly narrow-minded. Zofia still fondly remembers how Hilde translated letters to her family into

German in such a subtle way that the recipients were able to read between the lines, and that she did it all for free, without even asking for the traditional, compulsory ration of bread in return. She didn't act like you, because she couldn't stand conflict. She says to me: 'I knew that if I didn't do my best to help people, then there would be nothing left…'

Hilde tells me a lot about her life before Birkenau. In particular, she tells me about how the time spent in her Zionist organization in a particularly hostile environment, 1930s' Germany, had better equipped her than many of her comrades to be able to survive. It seems she was one of the few girls in the orchestra with whom Alma would interact a little more than usual. They talked about music, painting, and literature, but they also talked about the future. Alma gently mocked her ideal of the Promised Land in Palestine, and instead encouraged her to become the director of the orchestra she was planning on forming after the war with the girls from the group. By this time, however, Hilde was already too independent to be heavily influenced by Alma's views and opinions on life. Still, she clearly loved and admired her, and after moving to Israel, she's been reading everything she can about Gustav Mahler in order to better understand Alma.

*   *   *

Among her papers, Hilde also keeps Alma's last poem, written shortly before her death. Like most of her former comrades, she has her own personal feelings on Alma's passing, and is always moved when she speaks of it. As for myself, at each mention of Alma's death, in many ways emblematic by its unjust and mysterious character, I find similarities with how I feel about yours; the same throat, fists and teeth clenched with pain and helplessness.

Birkenau, March – April 1944

Alma isn't doing well. She's been complaining of severe migraines for several weeks, and from time to time asks Fania to massage her neck and head, hoping for some relief. It doesn't seem to be working. She complains constantly, amazing the girls who've never seen her like this before. She's downcast and depressed; Margott even saw her leaning against the bunker wall during a concert, pale and defeated. Despite this, she continues to demand great things from the orchestra and herself, and everyone begins to get used to seeing her mournful, thoughtful and silent.

In March she decides to set a strange poem she wrote to music. The piece in question is a piano study by Schumann, and is the same one that Serge Gainsbourg would use many years later for his song, *Un zeste de citron* (Lemon Incest).

> A song resonates within me
> A beautiful song
> that awakens memories in my soul
> My heart was still
> Now sweet sounds ring out again
> and awaken everything inside of me
> Life was distant and far away
> My heart, for a long time was so still
> And yet, now and near me
> All my happiness and desires
> My deepest aspirations and incessant fears
> They all come back to life
> All I want is for my heart to be still
> I yearn only for silence
> I no longer wish to think
> of a beautiful song.[15]

---

15. Translated from the original German.

In mir klingt ein Lied
ein schönes Lied
und durch die Seele mir Erinnern zieht
mein Herz war still
nun erklingen wieder zarte Töne
ruft in mir alles auf.   —
Leben war fern
und Wünsche fremd
mein Herz wie ruhig warst Du lange Zeit
doch nun kam nah
all mein Glück und mein Verlangen
tiefstes Sehnen schlaflos Bangen. —
Alles, alles lebt jetzt wieder auf
Ich will doch nur
Frieden für mein Herz
Ruhe will ich nur
nicht denken
an ein schönes Lied.

Alma's poem, written in Hilde's handwriting.

It's an astonishing request from a musician; to be willing to give up hearing music in exchange for peace. In contrast, Anita would confide years later that she would play concertos in order to keep her spirits up. For people like Alma, who wasn't only unable to adapt to the reality of Birkenau but, on the contrary, for a time even tried to submit to the reality of it, it was an act of denial.

The poem was originally to be sung to a Chopin study, but it was never made public. The themes of peace and nostalgia for times gone by were taboo under the Third Reich, and in Birkenau it was '*strengst verboten*' (strictly forbidden).

On 2 April, Alma is invited to a party hosted by Elza Schmidt, the *Kapo* of the *Bekleidungskammer*, (clothing warehouse) to celebrate her birthday. She can't refuse the request. After all, she has a rank to keep and "social" obligations to respect. After the party, Alma returns to the Block suffering increasing amounts of pain. A violent fever seizes her during the night and the next day, with a temperature of almost 40°C (104°F), she is violently ill and suffers from vomiting and migraines. Powerless to help, the girls rush to bring the doctor from the *Revier*. Alma's body is dotted with livid then bluish spots, and her temperature drops suddenly. No one can make sense of the symptoms, while Alma, still conscious, talks about what happened at the party the night before. Despite being a teetotaller, she'd drunk a little vodka or whatever its substitute was meant to be. No doubt an alcohol that had been distilled in the camp, which had then been tampered with and adulterated.

After being admitted to the *Revier*, her stomach is pumped but to no avail. Suspecting meningitis, the doctors then carry out a lumbar puncture to verify their diagnosis. The operation is extremely painful and she's completely unconscious throughout, yet she convulsively moves her head from side to side, as if, wherever she is in her mind, she can still feel the pain. Unable to agree on a diagnosis, the doctors discuss the possibility of sepsis. Not knowing what to do, they prescribe treatment to support her failing heart.

During the night of 4 April 1944, watched over by one of her friends, a doctor from the *Revier*, Alma is seized with convulsions that become closer and closer and more violent. At last, she calms down. It's over. The small window of harmony that Alma had managed to open in her time at Birkenau is closed.

*   *   *

Unique in the history of the camp, the authorities order Alma's body to be displayed on a kind of catafalque made from stools, covered with a white sheet. Someone places a branch of leaves on her body, and the orchestra is allowed to parade in front of her to bid her farewell. It's a last mark of respect from the Nazis to the person they called "Frau Alma" (Mrs Alma), perhaps the only one of the detainees not to be known by their number. However, it still doesn't prevent her body from being burned in the crematorium, just like the bodies of the most obscure little Jewish seamstresses from Budapest, Paris or Thessaloniki. This tribute paid to the renowned and talented artist is followed by the outrage that has been repeated a million times over. After all, Alma's body is still that of a Jew, and this is Birkenau.

Alma's death quickly fuels various contradictory and unverifiable rumours. Her position and status in the camp meant she had enemies, and Yvette and Lily are convinced she was poisoned. Alma had reportedly said she'd soon be leaving Birkenau to play with an orchestra at the front and entertain the troops. Jealous, Elza Schmidt, whom the Germans called "Pouf-Mama" (Madam Mother) must have poisoned her at the party. Margott also recalls another incident that took place shortly before Alma died, but that had nothing to do with *Kapo* Schmidt's famous birthday party.

The chief *Kapo* in the women's camp, the *Lagerältester*, who was a terrible, vulgar and violent woman, allegedly demanded to sing a Viennese song with the orchestra, with the intention of employing rather saucy lyrics. Realizing what she had in mind, Alma reportedly stopped the music and told the orchestra to return to their Block. Summoned before the authorities the next day, it was several hours before Alma emerged, staggering, and was taken directly to the *Revier*. Despite this, the majority of the girls believed Alma had died of meningitis, or poisoning, but this time due to drinking adulterated alcohol.

Alma's sudden death from unknown causes – no autopsy is allowed – creates shockwaves. Yet in Birkenau, death is far from mysterious. The exact opposite, in fact, as it's the whole site's primary objective. People are gassed, hanged, injected in the heart with phenol by executioners disguised as nurses, tortured and beaten to death. They die of typhus, dysentery, exhaustion and a thousand other things. People throw themselves on the electrified barbed wire, sometimes out of desperation, but also because they want to retain ultimate control and decide for themselves when and how they're going to die. But people don't die from unknown or inexplicable causes. For once, the Nazis have been cheated in their role as administrators of industrial and inhuman death.

Alma's death causes a crisis that the Nazis need to resolve swiftly; what will happen to the orchestra? Kramer, the head of the camp, doesn't want to deprive himself of this "service", and so quickly appoints Sonia Vinogradova, a Russian pianist, in her place.

*   *   *

Both Hilde and Regina had spoken to me of hope, of having something to strive for, without which survival seemed impossible. Hilde expressed it a rather striking way: 'With no hope of survival, all we could do was recite the *Shema Yisrael*, the prayer for the dying, the *Kaddish*, the prayer for the dead, and then throw ourselves on the barbed wire. It was a difficult decision to make, but it meant a swift end to the ongoing suffering.' Regina put it differently, although it was no less difficult to hear: 'I thought about throwing myself on the barbed wire, but then I saw the sun, and I wanted to live.'

And you? How did you try to make sense of it all? How did you plan to survive? Was it a longing, a desire to give life to an unborn child that helped you overcome the cold, hunger and fear? Was I already there somewhere in your mind or body, nothing more than a little speck?

For me, your absence in the recollections of these three women, and the ubiquitous character of Alma, is very confusing. I thought this absence would explain your transparency, the vagueness that I thought I knew so well. As a result, I very nearly put Alma in your place in my research and in my first draft, because of the way they almost all said how they owed their lives to her. I had identified myself so much with you and everything you were that after mingling it all together in this being called "the orchestra", I absorbed this symbolic position of nurturing and protective mother that I saw Alma occupying and allowed myself to become a part of it. I pictured Alma, a mother to you all and, feeling amalgamated with your group, was able to "adopt" and love her as my own mother. The added bonus was that it meant I could take you out of the camp, out of history. Instead, I could finally let you be a mother who was reliable, always present, and always admired, despite her weaknesses or excesses, but I wasn't quite ready to let go of this madness quite yet.

Chapter 12

Sylvia

Rehovot, Israel, May 1997

Hilde and Regina have already told me their story. Now it's Sylvia's turn. A very small woman, lively and petulant like quicksilver, she speaks quickly, precisely, and in a very confident manner. It's a sonorous voice, full of laughter. She has a deadly sense of humour and it's immediately obvious that she isn't used to feeling sorry for herself, even though she's just been released from hospital after having a hip operation. Was it another consequence from being in the camps, cancer, or some kind of nervous disease? No, it's "only" a relatively minor joint problem.

She resumed her studies in her fifties and now has a doctorate in science. It's another way, perhaps, of reweaving links with the past, her ruined childhood, interrupted schooling, and three-quarters of her adolescence destroyed.

* * *

Sylvia tells me about the rage she felt in the summer of 1987, in Germany. Invited by the city of Berlin, along with other Israelis who were born there before the war, she was due to attend the opening of a Jewish communal school. In attendance were representatives from the municipality, as well as members of the Berlin Jewish community, and everyone was happy and enthusiastic. The opening of the school was an extraordinary event and was a source of happiness and pride for all. For Sylvia, however, whose patience was never her finest quality, it was a time for her to bite back her tongue, angry and bitter at the fact that there should need to be such an occasion in the first place. Here was a Jewish primary school being opened, but fifty years earlier all schools and institutions for Jewish children were being closed. All of the children were deported, and Sylvia herself had been thrown out onto the streets, only managing to survive thanks to a succession of "miracles". Hilde and her husband had also attended the ceremony and remember it well, especially seeing Sylvia on the verge of exploding and narrowly avoiding what would've been a great scandal.

*   *   *

We're often interrupted by a parrot during our interview. It sings at the top of its voice, imitates the ringing of the telephone, calls everyone an idiot, and barks at the lap dog who's also there keeping us company. At one point I even think it sings the opening bars of Smetana's *Moldau*, or the *Hatikva*, the Israeli national anthem which was inspired by it. All in all, he behaves like a perfectly rude bird, and from time to time Sylvia answers him back, mockingly scolding him, rather proud of the effect he has.

A great deal of time has passed from what Sylvia experienced, and it shows. She often speaks coldly, as if talking about someone else's story, and I realize that the unease I feel isn't about what she's telling me, or the way she's doing it. No, the uneasiness I feel stems from the fact that I still don't know where or how to situate myself in this story. I'm not just an observer-narrator, because although she can't remember you, you're still somewhere there, right on the edge of the facts she describes to me. I can never really be fully involved either, as was never there...

Dessau, 30 January 1933

Sylvia Wagenberg is 6 years old on the day that Hitler becomes chancellor of Germany. Her first experience of Nazism takes place that same day. A fierce Nazi supporter who runs the cutlery factory not far from her house, celebrates the event in his own way by donning his brown uniform, putting on his red swastika armband, and adjusting his cap to give himself a martial air. All the props used by this sinister circus that will soon drag Europe into the abyss. He approaches Sylvia's mother and tells her 'If I catch your daughter, I'll slit her throat...' Sylvia is terrified. After all, he has huge cutlasses, meat slicers, scissors of all shapes and sizes on hand, all the tools necessary to carry out his threat... and Sylvia only has a tiny neck.

Since then, the little girl has avoided walking past the Nazi's shop, until the day he finally gets his hands on her. Unable to fight back, he holds her tight against him with one hand, and in the name of the defence of the German *Volk*, he slits the throats of the kittens that Sylvia had rescued.

* * *

Wanting to keep Sylvia and her sister Carla away from the city, their mother puts them both in a boarding school for young middle-class Jewish girls near Potsdam, a wealthy Berlin suburb. The girls remain there, quiet and semi-protected, until *Kristallnacht* in November 1938, when an enraged crowd destroys everything in the boarding school. Supposedly acting in the name of *Kultur* (culture) and European values, the barbarians even go so far as to throw the piano out into the courtyard.

The girls all leave for Berlin that same night, the smallest by train, the others on foot. When Sylvia and her sister arrive they see the disaster unfolding before them; the Jewish quarter of the city is already in flames. Their own house is right in the centre of town, on the corner of the Kürfürstendam, and the corner store is on fire. At this point in her life, Sylvia is like a sparrow, small and tiny, the archetypical physical representation of what the Nazis hate, with her slim face, huge shiny black eyes, and long black hair. Walking one day with her mother, she accidentally brushes against a man in a Nazi uniform. Convinced that the child had consciously tried to "infect" him, the Nazi immediately became enraged: 'How dare a Jew touch me!' he says, before resorting to expletives.

A few months later, her mother places Sylvia in an orphanage at Berlin-Alexanderplatz. She intends to leave the country for England, alone, leaving Carla and Sylvia behind; one in a Zionist youth camp, the other in the orphanage, under the tutelage of the headmistress. The two sisters already have more ties to their respective circle of friends than to each other, and it's during this time that Carla bonds with Hilde. Every day on her long walk to school, Sylvia is harassed by children dressed in the uniform of the Hitler Youth, but learns to avoid them by hiding in houses along the route.

*   *   *

The orphanage and Jewish high school are closed in 1942, and the children are all deported to Riga. Here they're initially locked up in the ghetto, before being massacred shortly afterwards in the Rumbula Forest. Sylvia is the only one to remain in Berlin. Having learned of the looming roundup, her tutor makes her leave the boarding school just in time and Sylvia will proceed to live with her for nearly a year. She helps out by delivering special letters from Jewish social institutions, announcing to Jewish families that they're going to be "transported" to the East.

During the year she spends living with her tutor, Sylvia is surrounded entirely by old people, members of Berlin's Jewish community, her guardian, and the people she contacts every day in the course of her work. She soon learns that two transports are due to leave the city. One, containing the "influential" members of the community, is bound for Theresienstadt in Czechoslovakia. The other, with young people gathered by the Nazis from all over Germany, will be transported to a place called Auschwitz.

Sylvia has had enough of the old people, and prepares to leave with the convoy of people her own age. They'll have to be sneaky, so the tutor says she'll pretend to stop Sylvia, and take her to the other meeting place instead. Auschwitz. Sylvia laughs when she tells me that she somehow ended up in Birkenau on her own initiative, of her own free will.

Several weeks later, in Birkenau, and admitted to hospital with furunculosis, Syliva hears a small voice calling out to her: 'Syliva!' It's her tutor, newly transferred from Theresienstadt. However, a "selection" will mean she'll soon be bound for the gas chamber.

Epilogue

Paris, August 1997
I finish dismantling a big, complicated, imaginary machine: I've done it to avoid looking for you, in the warren of my emotions, and in the labyrinth of other people's memories. The machine is this book. It's a way of implementing a fantasy I've always had of getting you out of Birkenau, or of trying to replace your ghost, at least, and one that doesn't have to bother with historical consistency or chronology.

It's helped to define my position on fatherhood. If I'd had a child, a link in the chain of generations between you and your grandchild, it would've forced me to talk about you. But what would I say when I'd refused to see you, my own mother?

It's also probably affected my relationship with music since I started playing. After all, weren't you a musician once? So I had to be able to audition for that too, to replace you and save your life. It finally defined my position vis-à-vis you. You became a project, whilst I became a researcher and investigator. It meant I was able to shelter myself from the emotional storms that otherwise might have surfaced within me following your comrades' revelations about your life, and about you, in the depths of hell.

For a year, during the time it took me to build your imaginary book, I gradually took your place, then that of an anonymous member of the orchestra who watched you from the side lines, all the while saying that I no longer wanted or needed to return to Birkenau in order to find my own identity.

But in reality, it wasn't about going back. I was already there, both you and me, in complete confusion. How could I get into such a mess? And also, how do I get myself out of it?

*   *   *

Here I am at the base of the wall. The real axis of this story, of this adventure, was never the orchestra, nor Alma: it was the two of us. In the end, I'll have to accept that in order to make my peace with your disappearance, to free myself from your deportation and your hidden suffering, I needed to find you. Although I travelled through Birkenau in my mind when your comrades were telling me their stories, when I finally went there in person it was to verify that you didn't exist there anymore, and that my story couldn't start there because nothing could ever start there. I wasn't born there, and there's nothing of me in that place at all. I don't need to lock myself in there on purpose to redeem some sort of error that neither you nor I made.

Strangely enough, I now realise that through the course of my quest for testimonies from your comrades, I followed the same route as you did, travelling to Belgium, Germany, Poland, France and the United States, where your life ended and where I found my sister, and Israel, where there was talk of transferring your body after your death.

It's become natural for me to try to release you after holding on to you so tightly for so long. I know that throughout my life I've wrongly interpreted the meaning and value of yours, the life that you were trying to rebuild with all your courage, and your illusions of a romantic little girl who fought against the odds, and even a little against us too.

For years I fought against the idea that had defined me for too long; that Birkenau was where I came from. I'm only now beginning to see the implications of this fight, and I feel – surprisingly – that

I'm no longer walking upside down, but on my legs, upright and in place. I need to break what it was that locked you in Birkenau even after your liberation, which came like a rebirth the day after your 22nd birthday. This scandalous period turned into something almost foundational for us, for me; a time and a place in which you remained fixed. And it was by this yardstick I measured your life, your death and, incidentally, my own.

You should have fought harder over the years that were left to you, to explain the reasons why you chose to live the way you did. I finally understand the struggle and pain it must have taken for you to refuse to submit to what you were expected to be, and for what you remained; a perpetual survivor, one forever cemented by the representations of others.

Putting your particular journey back into the frame of time means finally accepting that you didn't remain in Birkenau, you simply passed through it. Birkenau scarred you, bodily and psychologically, but it neither broke nor shaped you. As far as your family was concerned, Mengele would've said that you wouldn't live long. But for me, you're no longer this pathetic creature with a fate determined by the prediction of Nazi filth. You were everything Nazism aimed to eliminate: a woman and a Jew, and you also became a mother. You infuriated the Nazis, and even though you died too soon, I salute and respect your victory, and I am grateful to you.

In what I can now call my quest to find you, I know very well that I couldn't help but imagine your life in that place. I followed in your footsteps and looked over your shoulder in my writing, all so that I, too, could escape from Birkenau. And I finally understand that it was possible, helpful, vital even, to do so. You were a woman, and even though you're no longer here, I found you and accepted you in me, in spite of the fact I'd always denied you were there. I have within me – among other things – both a woman and a death that I must learn to live with. You can rest in peace, and I can finally make you speak, in my own words.

Paris, evening of 6 September 1948

Well, there it is. Here you are at last, my little man.

Tonight, everything is jostling around in my head, and yet I also feel that my mind's never been so clear. Your birth wasn't easy, and every bout of pain it caused me, that scalpel which opened my stomach, nevertheless helped me to be more on your side, because these birth pains were also pains of life, and they quickly faded when I first held you close to me, so tightly. Perhaps this means I'll be able to complete my transition from hell to a more acceptable place, a world where I can belong again.

Before you arrived, I still lived a bit like a stranger, an anachronism, an aberration of that time, a monster even; I felt worn out, tired and aged by several millennia despite my twenty-five calendar years. That period where I'd flown so close to death every second for two years, it's only now I realize how long it took for those feelings to pass, and how much it put me at odds with normal, living people, those for whom the present, past and the future had some sort of meaning and direction.

*   *   *

My return from that place wasn't easy, and I often had the impression – and still have it sometimes – that I'm constantly coming back from there, with my bowl, my spoon, my striped outfit, and my rucksack on my back. After the physical shock of returning to reality – to life beyond the barbed wire – I had the illusion that I'd only need a little time and a great deal of family care to get back into the flow of a more gentle life and sunnier times.

Our family was dispersed to the four corners of the globe. The person I still called my mother was somewhere in France. My brothers were hidden somewhere in Belgium. My grandparents, my surviving uncles and aunts, all exiles in England, Palestine, Tunisia or elsewhere. My world that had existed before the disaster unfolded had been shattered, and the word "future" no longer had much relevance. The inner devastation I'd suffered was reflected in the rubble the recent tornado had left in the people and places I knew before. Rubbish, rubble, everything came together without my even understanding how. It wasn't a peaceful happiness, just a coherent one.

I found my brothers, who'd become men in my absence. I found my mother, too, who'd abandoned us for seven years, with a new husband for her and a new sister for us. There was a tacit contract between all of us that we would no longer speak of the one who had disappeared in Poland, your grandfather. We never even spoke about whether we missed him; the illusion of unity we were living under would probably have cracked if we did. The places of my childhood had all been swept away, materially at least, by bombs and shells. The Germany that I thought was my homeland was dead to me, thanks to the memory I retained of its fall into horror.

Worse still, people lowered their voices around me when certain things were mentioned. I was treated like I was still sick or helpless. Everyone's little delicacies, unasked questions, false modesty and attentiveness weighed heavily on me and hurt me, making it all the more difficult for me to move on. But in fact, the dance of death swirled in my head to the sound of the music I heard, the Beautiful Blue Danube *and the barking of the attack dogs,* Rigoletto *and the selections on the ramp,* Carmen *and the gas chambers…*

I have to learn to redo the motions of everyday life – washing, dressing, putting on make-up, going shopping, looking for work – without really living in the moment, so that after a while they gradually begin to feel more real, and I can finally climb up and out from the abyss and start drifting with the others again, albeit a little heavier than everyone else.

*   *   *

That's sort of why I hid my violin at the back of a cupboard, because it gave me the impression of images I never wanted to see again; the sight of inmates stretching out unendingly, our music repeating itself over and over again endlessly, my friends, sisters, dying that day or the day before, their bodies piled in heaps like rubbish, and our executioners, these dogs, who could be both informed music lovers and at the same time the efficient organizers of our distress...

I know that in burying a piece of wood under some clothes, like some form of exorcism, I won't magically succeed in cancelling out these monstrosities that I've witnessed. I'm not as naive as people think me to be.

In spite of everything, I have the strong sense that I'll probably never play the violin again. Before that time it always represented beauty and peace, but now, it can never mean joy, happiness or delight again. How can I hear the Barcarolle *from* The Tales of Hoffmann *or* Madame Butterfly *without imagining my comrades looking at us, some with anger, contempt or pity, others with tears in their eyes, all silent as the dead, pressed up behind the barbed wire during one of our Sunday concerts?*

I wish the shell that I used to protect myself in order to survive and not fall into madness didn't cling to me so much. I wasn't insensitive – none of us was – just tense, and it still hurts that I had to harden myself that way. Being forced to save myself meant cutting myself off from the rest of the world, what we used to call "the real world" in there. The lingering smell of mass graves and death can permeate everything; because it's contagious, it scares people and keeps them away. I'm still not completely cleansed of all of this. My biggest failure and biggest pain would be that, in turn, it permeates you and takes you away from me.

However, it seems to me that everything is finally starting to mend. Your reddened, wrinkled face, your carrot hair, your round blue eyes and your fourteen inches of life demand love and attention that will carry me out of the house of the dead and into the open air towards real life, if I can give you enough strength to pull me towards you.

*   *   *

You slept quietly in your cradle that first night, a few steps away from me. Your little fists already a little clenched, your forehead wrinkled slightly during this first sleep. What was bothering you, my baby boy? Did you share my own uncertainties and anxieties while I was waiting for you to arrive? Did you have a little aerial pointed at me? Did you see those horrific visions as they passed through my mind, even though they're now already slightly blurred and distorted when I look at you? Right now you can't really know everything about what you represent to me, what future you personify, what reparations you symbolize.

I sense it's not going to be easy for you to be the vessel, the symbol, of my return to the living. I'll try with all my might not to use you as an anchor too much to secure me to a more peaceful existence. I already know it'll be a burden for you, we can't escape that, but I'll help you all I can to live with it, although you'll probably have to help me help you, too. My already innocent baby, to be born with such a burden! Unlike so many new-born babies who call on their mothers all of the time, you stay calm and silent. The tranquillity of your sleep, your calmness on this first day of life, are they the first means you've found of protecting me by leaving me in peace? Do you already know something about me that I don't? Have you ever felt what it is that makes me so worried, that I might not be worthy, that I might not be the mother you need?

I keep hearing about wars all the time, about the one I lived through, but also those that may still come. Like all of us, I hoped that our suffering, our past misery, could at least be used to teach others a lesson, to show what you risk when you march past in single file to military music, and begin to take pleasure in preying on old people and children.

Indeed, a few months after our return, when Auschwitz and Belsen had left the front pages, and when the shocking images of what we had experienced in everyday life had faded, everything went back to how it was before, just as it did after the First World War. Throughout the world we continue to kill, burn, and bomb others, all with calamitous justifications, and even in the name of Peace. And it hurts me all the more that now you're also threatened by those barbarians to come, as well.

From time to time, I see people demonstrating in the street, veterans, and ex-deportees alike. Having mended, washed and ironed their uniforms, they put them on again and in some cases, it acts as a disguise, hiding the cracks beneath, because luckily for them they've started to put on a little weight once more. As for me, the mere sight of stripes on a fabric always revolts me and revives images that I'd prefer to leave where they are.

Was it selfish and completely reckless of me to decide to give birth to a baby at such a time, when the future looks so dark? For a little while, as you grew inside me and I waited for you to arrive, I got scared. I was afraid of not knowing how to protect you, afraid of not being up to the task of surviving the impossible a second time if it all happened again, afraid that you'd be marked by this fear, and all my previous ones.

It's a fear that's probably as indelible as the tattoo I wear on my left arm. Back then I was alone; it was only my life that was in danger – one of millions – but it was already a struggle for me to hang on and keep holding on. I was pretty dependent on others at the time, those who were helping me as well as those I was trying to help. Not like you, who depend almost completely on me now. Your existence adds value to my own, but I'm not sure it makes me fight more. I don't think I have that in me; I'm just someone who survived by chance. If another disaster befalls us, if the Beast arises again, all I ask is to be able to cope once again, for you and for your father.

However, whatever the future may have in store for you, when I look at you and hold you in my arms, I know that I was right to take this chance. I'm proud of my decision and, for a little while, I'm almost at peace with myself, and the concept of unhappiness recedes somewhat.

*   *   *

Is this the happiness I dreamed of back then? That excitement you feel when packing your suitcase before a holiday, and a vague sense of contentment knowing you're not quite alone anymore? How I dreamed of this moment! I'd gone through all of that to give you life, just forty or so months after my return. It's all still an unfathomable mystery to me. I'm aware of the incredible luck I've had, and I also know how many of us, the anonymous and the destitute, won't have had any at all. I'm going to do my best to work as hard and as best as I can, for you, and for me. You're worth it, and I think I deserve it.

I'm sure that you and your father are the best things to have happened to me in a long time. I'd hardly dared hoped for such a thing before, because it was always too painful. And I know it's thanks to you that I've managed to find the resources inside of me to not let myself sink back into that state. Dreaming of a husband who finds me beautiful, and of a baby who thinks I'm a good mother, might have been the flicker of hope that allowed me to overcome the shame that we all live with daily.

Oddly enough, during the period when I was waiting for you, I often thought about my childhood, before the war, when I had no idea that anyone could want to harm me, since I had no desire to harm anyone else. I saw myself as a little girl, very young, wise beyond her years, without a loving father and a mother who wasn't always around. My brother was my only guide, while school and music were my only support in what was a very monotonous existence, troubled only by our movements through a Europe where the Nazi gangrene was gaining ground daily.

What revenge it would be for all of us, the living as well as the dead, not to make you experience the same things, so that your very survival doesn't punctuate your days, your fears don't accompany you constantly, and your nightmares don't haunt you. On the contrary, I want you to be free, strong, funny and good-natured – everything we didn't know how to be and that it's time you were!

How I wish I could give you that feeling of being joyful and carefree, with songs like the ones I haven't sung for years, and the silly games and nursery rhymes in all the languages I know. Unfortunately, even if I still know how to sing, even for you, I'm no longer sure I'll have the resources within me to do so. If we started dancing around to nursey rhymes, I'm afraid I'd be dancing on mass graves at the same time.

*   *   *

Your grandfather who never returned, my father, whom I last saw when they came to take us away, and who was later replaced by another man alongside my mother, you're going to have to keep him alive a little longer, as I wanted to give you his name, hidden, as a middle name. It's the one last thing I can do for him, even though remembering and thinking about him is painful for everyone. And it hurts me that I can't do more.

I wish I could've protected him more, when my mother left us alone shortly before the disaster. I wanted to save him so much when they came to get us, I was even willing to give my own life instead. I felt so helpless and useless at the time, too fearful to hold back the barbarians who were taking us away, too weak or too foolish to invent a new way to free him. I could only share his fate, but not to the end.

What guilt am I atoning for now? What trial am I being subjected to? Was I so bad that I wasn't able to escape their clutches? Rather, am I making amends for my biggest sin; that of having preferred to be with him, my father, once my mother, my competitor for his affections, had left the scene?

I can well imagine his last moments somewhere out there, but I don't want you to know anything of his failed life, nor his distorted and inhuman death. I'm going to strive to ensure that you know nothing of what I'm going through, and the price I'm now paying for my weaknesses and mistakes I made as a little girl and a teenager.

My little one, you can't do anything with these images of death that pass through my mind, the questions that haunt me, and the guilt that undermines me. They're just acid-like, crystallized evil. There's nothing good in them that we can share. I don't want you to have to wade through all this, and I'll forbid you from doing so for as long as I can.

Perhaps by keeping this secret to myself, I'm creating a silence between the two of us that we might end up paying dearly for. This silence — like lead — seems more preferable to me than remembering my two years away from the world of the living, and what I became as a result. Why should I burden you with it? Why should I burden anyone? It's my responsibility, it's what I believe is best for you, and it's my choice in my role as a mother.

And yet although I know it's necessary, I'm sad to have already created a division, an insurmountable barrier, between us. Yet that's how it must be. This period of my life, and everything I did in order to preserve it, will forever be inaccessible to you.

*   *   *

When I returned, I didn't know your grandfather was missing. Nor did I know our lovely Lydia was missing, too, along with her parents. The extent of what had happened only emerged gradually, and I began to wonder if I had the right to be a survivor. I had to pull myself together so as not to fall down. I thought I could see some sort of reproach in every glance, a demand for justification in every question.

As I got off the train in Brussels after my return from Germany, every photograph I was handed, every human face I saw there, each parent, brother, husband who asked me if I had seen their loved ones (although how was I supposed to match these old photographs with the standing corpses that we'd become?), threw as many silent accusations in my face as I had of my own. Why was I there when there were others still waiting, no longer really even believing their family members were alive, yet still wanting to believe in miracles?

Despite the great happiness your birth has given me, I'm still not at peace. The visions of my time there will continue to haunt me for a long time to come, especially at night. Your father knows a little about this, woken as he is by my nightmares, which are always the same. A dimly lit station platform, the puffing of the locomotive, my father and little cousin lost somewhere where I can't find them, in a group of prisoners jumbled together in a cattle wagon; two girls next to me, fighting like wolves for a piece of fat they've found by chance at the bottom of a pot, and me, stuck there, unable to separate them; a column of striped shadows, including myself, which crawls under a sky of ash; and this oily, omnipresent smoke that permeates right through me to the last atom, to my final dream.

This is how, my little one, certain people, who I can almost call our equals, wanted me dead. They saw me as a pest, like a bug or a cockroach that needs to be eliminated to keep everything clean and disinfected. Can you hate a person the same way you would hate an insect? No. In their indifferent, professional manner they established all the necessary technical procedures and set up all the machines so that I would die anonymously, in the shit and the mud; if they failed, then it's only by the barest of margins, and I'm still scarred by their attempt.

Oh yes, my little boy, I'm not, and will never be, the most beautiful mother in the world; everything I should've been, pure, naive, full of youthful confidence, it all flew away thanks to my two years in hell. Perhaps I'll never get it back. The scars are too deep.

How am I going make sure, day after day, that you're not overloaded with everything that burdens me? I'm not yet able, or willing, to speak about it to anyone other than my former companions, my sisters, Fanny, Hélène. How could I possibly want or know how to discuss it with those who don't understand it? How could they understand me? It's almost as if I've arrived from another planet, another passage in time, where we don't even speak the same language. What does my hunger and theirs, my fears and theirs, my fatigue and theirs have in common, apart from the mere sound of those empty words? What could they know of the eternal nights that seemed to flow through an hourglass, as my life slowly dissolved, second after second?

It might even be a relief for me to open up, to loosen the noose that grips tightly around my neck. Is it worth me waking up those feelings deep inside me, and risk making my loved ones miserable by overwhelming them with it all? In the end, there's nothing they can do to help, except perhaps half kill me with their disbelief, or worse, with their pity.

Like a knot of suffering and unanswered questions, there's still something there I can't quite put my finger on. Sometimes it grips me fiercely, like a cramp, and other times it cuts me like an open wound and refuses to go away. Perhaps it's time to break this chain that imprisons me, link by link. My marriage, your birth, your demands, perhaps they'll re-teach me optimism – yet another burden for you, my son! Will there come a day when I no longer have to sacrifice myself for others, nor depend on them, however close they may be? And although you can do nothing about it, do I risk passing on this awkward situation to you?

There's only one thing I can do from now on. Even though I no longer pray, I must pray that you have the time and space to grow up as far away as possible from the horror, guilt and confusion. I'll hold on to what oppresses me, and risk living in that place between you, who represents everything that is real, the only thing I care about in my life, and my visions, my nightmares, and my imagined death. I just hope you'll be strong enough to pull me over to your side.

Don't move, don't do anything that might disturb the pain; like a toothache that goes away when you fall asleep, but you know will return when you awake, yet still cling to the belief that it'll go away on its own, like a fire that runs out of fuel. Perhaps by paying this price I'll be able to ensure that you, my son, and that you, my husband, won't share that taste of ash that still lingers in my mouth.

Members of the Women's Orchestra of Auschwitz[16]

CONDUCTOR

ZOFIA TCHAÏKOWSKA	Polish	April '43	Aug '43	
Blockowa until January '45				
ALMA ROSÉ	Austrian	Aug '43		Jewish
Died at Birkenau			April '44	
SONIA VINOGRADOVA	Russian	April '44	Oct '44	
Piano then conductor			Jan '45	

VIOLIN

HÉLÈNE WIERNIK ('BIG HÉLÈNE')	Belgian	June '43	Oct '44	Jewish
HELENA DUNICZ	Polish	Oct '44	Jan '45	
LILI MATHÉ	Hungarian	July '43 (?)	Oct '44	Jewish
JADWIGA ('WISHA') ZATORSKA	Polish	April '43	Jan '45	Jewish
IRENA LAGOWSKA	Polish	June '43	Jan '45	
VIOLETTE ZYLBERSTEIN	French	May '43	Oct '44	Jewish
ELSA MILLER	Belgian	May '43	Oct '44	Jewish
ZOFIA CYKOWIAK	Polish	May '43	Jan '45	
HÉLÈNE ROUNDER ('LITTLE HÉLÈNE')	French	Sept '43	Oct '44	Jewish
IBI (?)	Hungarian	April '44		Jewish
Died at Birkenau		Sep '44 (?)		
JULIE STROUMZA ('LITTLE JULIE')	Greek	Aug '43 (?)		
Died at Birkenau			(?) '44	Jewish
'LITTLE FANNY'	French	(?) '43	Oct '44	Jewish

16. Due to lack of accurate information, not all orchestra members are included in this list.

OCCASIONAL VIOLIN

HENRYKA CZAPLA	Polish	June '43		
Transferred, according to Claude Torres			Sept '43	
HENRYKA GALAZKA	Polish	May '43		
Transferred, according to Claude Torres			Aug '43	
MARIA LAGENFELD	Polish	April '43	Aug '43	
HILDE GRÜNBAUM (then copyist)	German	April '43	Oct '44	Jewish

CELLO

MARIA KRONER	German	May '43		Jewish
Died at Birkenau			Aug '43	
ANITA LASKER	German	Nov '43	Oct '44	Jewish

DOUBLE BASS

YVETTE ASSAEL	Greek	May '43	Oct '44	Jewish

MANDOLIN

NASZA (?)	Polish	April '43	Dec '43	
RACHELA OLEWSKI	Polish	April '43	Oct '44	Jewish
FANNY KORNBLUM ('BIG FANNY')	Belgian	July '43	Oct '44	Jewish
OLGA (?)	Ukrainian	Aug '43	Jan '45	
BIG JULIE	Greek	April (?) '43	Oct '44	Jewish

OCCASIONAL MANDOLIN

KAZIMIERA MALYS	Polish	June '43	Aug '43	
MARIA MOS	Polish	April '43	Aug '43	
IRENA WALASZCZYK	Polish	June '43	Aug '43	
HELENA 'ZIPPY' TISCHAUER	Czech			Jewish
Died at Birkenau, according to Helena		(?) '43	(?) '43	

GUITAR

BRONIA (?)	Ukrainian	May '43	Jan '45 (?)	
SZURA (?)	Ukrainian	April '43	Jan '45 (?)	
MARGOTT VETROVCOVA	Czech	July '43	Oct '44	Jewish
SZTEFANIA BARUCH	Polish	April '43	(?)	Jewish

FLUTE

LOLA 'FRAU' or 'AUNT' KRONER	German	July '43	Oct '44	Jewish

RECORDER

RUTH BASSIN	German	April '43	Oct '44	Jewish
CARLA WAGENBERG	German	April '43	Oct '44	Jewish
SYLVIA WAGENBERG	German	April '43	Oct '44	Jewish

ACCORDIAN

ESTHER LÖWY Transferred to Ravensbrück	German	May '43	Aug '43	Jewish
LILLY ASSAEL	Greek	May '43	Aug '44	Jewish

FLORIA SCHRIJVERS
  Also Kramer's nanny for a
    number of weeks
	German	Aug '43	Oct '44	Jewish

PIANO

DANUTA (DANKA)
  KOLLAKOWA
  Then cymbals
	Polish	April '43	Jan '45	

ALA GRES	Russian	Dec '43 (?)	Jan '45	

PERCUSSION

HELGA SCHIESSEL	German	Aug '43	Oct '44	Jewish

SINGERS

MARIA BIELICKA	Polish	May '44	Jan '45	
CLAIRE MONIS	French	Jan '44	Oct '44	Jewish
DORYS (?) Died at Birkenau	German	Aug '43	Nov '43	Jewish
FANIA FÉNELON	French	Jan '44	Oct '44	
LOTTE LEBEDOWA	Czech	Aug '43	Oct '44	Jewish
ÉVA STOJOWSKA According to Helena	Polish	Nov '43	Nov '44	
JANINA KALICINSKA	Polish	Dec '44	Jan '45	
ÉVA STEINER	Hungarian	June '44 (?)	Oct '44	Jewish

ASSISTANT (*STUBENDIENST/STUBOWA*)

REGINA KÜPFEBERG	Polish	Aug '43 (?)	Oct '44	Jewish

OCCASIONAL ASSISTANT (*STUBENDIENST*)

SZTEFANIA (PANE FOUNIA), BARUCH, MARIA LANGENFELD
(until Jan '45)

COPYISTS

ALA GRES
FANIA FÉNELON
KAZIMIERA MALYS
MARIA MOS
REGINA KÜPFEBERG
MARGOTT VETROVCOVA
HILDE GRÜNBAUM